Gypsy

TITLES BY STEPHEN SONDHEIM
AVAILABLE FROM TCG

Assassins, book by John Weidman
Company, book by George Furth
Follies, book by James Goldman
Getting Away with Murder, co-authored with George Furth
Gypsy, book by Arthur Laurents
Into the Woods, book by James Lapine
Pacific Overtures, book by John Weidman
Passion, book by James Lapine

A MUSICAL

Gypsy

BOOK BY
Arthur Laurents

LYRICS BY
Stephen Sondheim

MUSIC BY
Jule Styne

SUGGESTED BY
THE MEMOIRS OF
GYPSY ROSE LEE

Theatre Communications Group • New York

Gypsy is published by Theatre Communications Group, Inc., 520 Eighth Ave., 24th Fl., New York, NY 10018-4156.

Publication of this edition of *Gypsy* was supported, in part, by the Opera-Musical Theater Program of the National Endowment for the Arts.

This publication is made possible in part with public funds from the New York State Council on the Arts, a State Agency.

TCG books are exclusively distributed to the book trade by Consortium Book Sales and Distribution, 1045 Westgate Dr., St. Paul, MN 55114.

LIBRARY OF CONGRESS CATALOGING-IN-PUBLICATION DATA
Styne, Jule, 1905–
  [Gypsy. Libretto]
  Gypsy: a musical (suggested by the memoirs of Gypsy Rose Lee) / book by
Arthur Laurents ; music by Jule Styne ; lyrics by Stephen Sondheim.—1st TCG ed.
  Libretto.
  ISBN 1-55936-086-0
  1. Musicals—Librettos. 2. Lee, Gypsy Rose, 1914–1970—Drama. I. Lee,
Gypsy Rose, 1914–1970. II. Laurents, Arthur. III. Sondheim, Stephen. IV. Title.
ML50.S955G9 1994
782.1'4'0268—dc20   94-2588
                                                              CIP MN

On the cover: *Gypsy* logo courtesy of RHI Entertainment, Inc.
Design and composition by The Typeworks

First TCG Edition, July 1994
Fourth Printing, February 2004

To Erna Fillmore,
the grandest maternal cannibal of them all

GYPSY *was first presented by David Merrick and Leland Hayward at The Broadway Theatre, New York City, May 21, 1959, with the following cast:*

(IN ORDER OF APPEARANCE)

UNCLE JOCKO	Mort Marshall
GEORGE	Willy Sumner
ARNOLD (and his guitar)	Johnny Borden
BALLOON GIRL	Jody Lane
BABY LOUISE	Karen Moore
BABY JUNE	Jacqueline Mayro
ROSE	Ethel Merman
POP	Erv Harmon
NEWSBOYS	Bobby Brownell, Gene Castle, Steve Curry, Billy Harris
WEBER	Joe Silver
HERBIE	Jack Klugman
LOUISE	Sandra Church
JUNE	Lane Bradbury
TULSA	Paul Wallace
YONKERS	David Winters
L.A.	Michael Parks
ANGIE	Ian Tucker
KRINGELEIN	Loney Lewis
MR. GOLDSTONE	Mort Marshall
MISS CRATCHITT	Peg Murray
FARMBOYS	Marvin Arnold, Ricky Coll, Don Emmons, Michael Parks, Ian Tucker, Paul Wallace, David Winters
HOLLYWOOD BLONDES	
AGNES	Marilyn Cooper
MARJORIE MAY	Patsy Bruder
DOLORES	Marilyn D'Honau
THELMA	Merle Letowt
EDNA	Joan Petlak
GAIL	Linda Donovan

COW	Willy Sumner and George Zima
PASTEY	Richard Porter
TESSIE TURA	Maria Karnilova
MAZEPPA	Faith Dane
CIGAR	Loney Lewis
ELECTRA	Chotzi Foley
SHOWGIRLS	Kathryn Albertson, Denise McLaglen,
	Barbara London, Theda Nelson,
	Carroll Jo Towers, Marie Wallace
RENÉE	Marsha Rivers
PHIL	Joe Silver
BOUGERON-COCHON	George Zima

Entire production directed and choreographed by
JEROME ROBBINS
Settings and lighting by Jo Mielziner
Costumes designed by Raoul Pène du Bois
Musical direction by Milton Rosenstock
Orchestrations by Sid Ramin *with* Robert Ginzler
Dance music arranged by John Kander
Additional dance music by Betty Walberg

The action of the play covers a period from the early twenties to the early thirties, and takes place in various cities throughout the country.

MUSICAL NUMBERS

ACT ONE

1. "May We Entertain You"

    BABY JUNE AND BABY LOUISE
2. "Some People"   ROSE
3. Traveling
4. "Small World"   ROSE AND HERBIE
5. Baby June and Her Newsboys
6. "Mr. Goldstone, I Love You"   ROSE AND ENSEMBLE
7. "Little Lamb"   LOUISE
8. "You'll Never Get Away from Me"   ROSE AND HERBIE
9. Dainty June and Her Farmboys
10. "If Momma Was Married"   LOUISE AND JUNE
11. "All I Need Is the Girl"   TULSA AND LOUISE
12. "Everything's Coming Up Roses"   ROSE

ACT TWO

1. "Madame Rose's Toreadorables"

    LOUISE and the HOLLYWOOD BLONDES
2. "Together, Wherever We Go"   ROSE, LOUISE
                                           AND HERBIE
3. "You Gotta Get a Gimmick"   TESSIE, MAZEPPA and
                                             ELECTRA
4. "Small World"—Reprise   ROSE
5. "Let Me Entertain You"   LOUISE and COMPANY
6. "Rose's Turn"   ROSE

ACT ONE

Scene One

On either side of the proscenium, there are illuminated placards—as in the days of vaudeville. After the overture, the placards light up to read:

UNCLE JOCKO'S KIDDIE SHOW
SEATTLE

The light illuminating the placards fades slowly as the curtain rises on the stage of a tacky vaudeville theatre.

The stage is half-set for the rehearsal of a kiddie show. "Uncle Jocko"—the nervous, oily master of ceremonies—is surrounded by a pack of babbling kids and their tigress mothers. The kids are in horrible, homemade costumes; the mothers wear clothes of the very early twenties; Jocko wears a tartan cap and fake horn-rimmed glasses as a concession to his name.

JOCKO: Everybody—SHUT UP!... All mothers—*out. (To his assistant)* Georgie, I don't want them in the wings, I don't want them in the theatre, I want them OUT!

GEORGIE: It's a pleasure. O.K., mothers—this way. Move it! *(He herds them out as—)*

JOCKO: All right, kids, get in a straight line along here and come forward one at a time. The doors open at seven and Uncle Jocko doesn't have enough time to rehearse your darlin' acts. *(He takes a simpering little girl completely covered*

3

with balloons out of line and moves her down, apart from the others) You wait here, girly-girl. *(Calling out front to the Spot Man)* Oh, Gus! Hit this doll with a surprise pink when she does her turn. *(To the girl)* Uncle Jocko promised the wee bairn would be a winner and she will. *(The kid kisses him coyly. To Georgie)* Chip off her sister's block. And you ought to see them balloons! O.K. Let's have the first wee laddie in Uncle Jocko's Kiddie Show.

(As a little boy with a big accordion comes forward, Jocko speaks to the actual Conductor in the pit)

Take each of them from the top and then cut to the last eight. Every Friday night, ya ta ta, ya ta ta, Uncle Jocko dinna ken there were so many talented bairns right here in Seattle and the rest of the crap—ARNOLD AND HIS ACCORDION! *(As Arnold plays—indicating the kid)* Georgie, that's what's gonna kill vaudeville. All right, Arnold, cut to the end. The end, kiddo.

(He signals the Conductor for a sick chord; Georgie pushes Arnold off. Jocko speaks to two little girls dressed as a Dutch boy and girl)

And who does Uncle Jocko have here? Who the hell does he—BABY JUNE AND COMPANY?...*(To the Conductor)* Half of the song, half of the dance, and off.

CONDUCTOR: Got ya.

(A small band starts the introduction)

JUNE *(Singing)*:
  May we entertain you?
  May we see you smile?
  I will do some kicks—

LOUISE *(Singing)*:
  I will do some tricks.

4

ROSE *(From out front)*: Sing out, Louise—sing out!

JOCKO: Who said that?

JUNE *(Singing)*:
　　I'll tell you a story.

LOUISE *(Singing)*:
　　I'll dance when she's done.

ROSE *(From front)*: You're behind, Louise! Catch up, honey, catch up!

JOCKO: Who let in one of them mothers?

JUNE, LOUISE:
　　By the time we're through
　　Entertaining you—

　　(Coming down the aisle and onto the stage, carrying a little dog and a big handbag is—momma!)

ROSE: Hold it, please, hold it! Save your strength, June. Louise, dear, if you don't count—

JOCKO: Madam, do you realize you are absolutely—

ROSE: I do, Uncle Jocko, but I want to save your very valuable time for you.

JOCKO: In that case—

ROSE: When I saw your sensitive face at the Odd Fellows Hall—my first husband was an Odd Fellow—

JOCKO: I am not an Odd Fellow!

ROSE: I meant a Knight of Pythias. My second husband was—

JOCKO: I'm not a Knight of Pythias!

ROSE: Then where *did* you catch our act?

JOCKO: At the Elks.

ROSE: My father is an Elk! I have his tooth here someplace. *(She dumps the dog into Jocko's arms as she rummages in her handbag)* If you'll just hold Chowsie for me—that's short for chow mein. *(Baby talk)* Mommy just loves chow mein, doesn't she, Chowsie Wowsie? Stop sucking your thumb,

5

Louise. *(To the Conductor)* Professor, I just marvel how you can make a performer into an artist.

JOCKO *(Following her as she gads about)*: What is going on here??

ROSE: Now if you could help my little girls by giving them a good loud la da *da* de da da *da—* *(To Jocko, whom she delicately shoves back as he moves to intervene)* God helps him who helps himself. *(To the Drummer)* Mr. Zipser—when the girls do their specialty would you please ad lick it? Show him, girls.

JOCKO: Is this really happening?!

ROSE: Oh, Gus? Gus, would you please slap Baby June with something pink? She's the star. Smile, Baby dear!

JOCKO: I have seen all kinds of mothers—

ROSE: Do you know of a really good agent—don't hang on the baby, Louise, you're rumpling her dress—who could book a professional act like ours?

JOCKO: A professional act! Hey, Georgie! Get a load of this crazy—

ROSE *(Suddenly grabbing him)*: Don't you laugh! *Don't you dare laugh!*... That child is going to be a star.

JOCKO: That's what they all say. All right— *(He shoves the dog back into her arms)*

ROSE: But we're not finished!

JOCKO: You are as far as I'm concerned.

ROSE: Because you're trying to play favorites!

JOCKO *(Stops)*: What?

ROSE: How dare you let that rotten, untalented fat balloon block up my babies? I won't leave this stage till she does!

JOCKO: That child—

ROSE: Have you no loyalty to the Elks?

JOCKO: I'm not an Elk!

ROSE: Well, the editor of the *Gazette is*! I happen to know because at the last meeting he showed my father a letter he got—complaining some contest was fixed... I guess desperate people do desperate things.

(Jocko stares at her, then motions the Balloon Girl to go. Rose looks at the Conductor, and signals him as before)

La da *da* de da *da!*

(Music starts and the girls begin their act)

Thank you, Professor. Thank you, Uncle Jocko. *(She gives him the dog)* Thank you, Gus! Thank you, Mr. Zipser! Smile, girls, smile!

(She is singing along with her girls when she sees the Balloon Girl, who has edged out from the wings. Still singing gaily, Rose removes her hatpin. The Balloon Girl backs into the wings as Rose marches after her, the hatpin extended like Joan of Arc's sword. Her dancing daughters watch, grin and finish to a blare of music)

(The lights black out)

Scene Two

The illuminated placards change to read:

"HOME SWEET HOME"

SEATTLE

The scene is the kitchen of a frame house. Later that night.

We see an icebox, a sink overflowing with dishes, calendars and timetables on the walls, a rocker, etc.

Louise and June enter yawning, and take off the coats they wear over their costumes as Rose slams in, throws her coat on a chair and heads for the icebox. She gives Chowsie, the little dog, to Louise as she gets a can of dog food from the icebox. As usual, she is talking all the time.

ROSE: That rotten little Uncle Jocko! He's as cheap as your grandpa. *(To June)* Ten bucks for a talent like yours! Well, we're through with Kiddie Shows. *And* with your grandpa's lodge hall. It's time we moved on anyway! I'm gonna get us an agent to book the act on the Orpheum Circuit.

LOUISE: That's dog food, Momma.

ROSE: That's what she thinks. I'm hungry.

LOUISE: Then why didn't you eat some of our chow mein after the show?

ROSE: Because you two did the work and we gotta save every cent. *(To June, who brings her a hair brush—as she brushes*

8

June's hair) I had a dream last night: a whole new act for you! Baby June and Her Newsboys!

JUNE: How are you going to get the boys, Momma?

ROSE: Louise can be a boy—

(Louise exits)

—and I'll find three others.

JUNE: How are you going to pay them?

ROSE: The experience'll be their pay. I've got just enough saved up for scenery and costumes. If I can squeeze a few bucks out of Grandpa, we can head for Los Angeles and the Orpheum Circuit . . .

(Pop enters. He is a crusty old man, holding the Bible he is eternally reading. A short pause)

JUNE *(Tactfully)*: Good night, Momma. Good night, Grandpa. *(She exits)*

POP: You oughta be ashamed: fooling your kids with those dreams!

ROSE: They're real dreams and I'm gonna make 'em *come* real for my kids!

POP: What are you, Rose, a crazy woman?! God put you down right here because He meant for you to stay right here!

ROSE: God's like me, Pop: we both need outside assistance.

POP: You've squeezed the last penny outa me that you're ever gonna get!

ROSE: It ain't for me! It's for my girls. It's too late for me.

POP: It ain't too late for you to get a husband to support you.

ROSE: After three husbands, I'm through with marriage. I want to enjoy myself. I want my girls to enjoy themselves and travel like Momma does!

POP: And you'll leave them just like your mother left you!

ROSE: Never! *(She turns to see Louise, who has entered behind her)* Why aren't you ready for bed, Louise?

LOUISE: June says you said she can sleep with you tonight.

9

ROSE: You know how high-strung the baby is after a performance.

LOUISE: I performed.

ROSE: It ain't the same. Now say good night and go to bed.

LOUISE: Good night, Grandpa. *(She kisses him)*

POP: Good night, Plug. You're a good girl.

ROSE: You *are* a good girl and I was proud of you tonight.

(Louise runs to her and hugs her)

LOUISE: Momma, how come I have three fathers?

ROSE: Because you're lucky.... You were born with a caul. That means you got powers to read palms and tell fortunes and wonderful things are going to happen for you!

(Louise goes)

POP: Why do you fill her with such bunk?

ROSE: It ain't bunk!

POP: Nothin' wonderful is going to happen to her or June—or to you.

ROSE: Maybe not to me, but they're gonna have a marvelous time! I'll be damned if I'm gonna let them sit away their lives like I did. And like you do—with only that calendar to tell you one day is different from the next! And that plaque—

(Pointing to a gold plaque on the wall)

—from your rotten railroad company to say congratulations: for fifty years, you did the same dull thing every dull day!

POP: That plaque is a great tribute! It's solid gold!

ROSE: How much could you get for it?

POP: Rose, if you—

ROSE: What good's it doin' sittin' there?!

POP: That plaque belongs there like you belong home—instead of running around the country like a Gypsy!

ROSE: Anybody that stays home is dead! If I die, it won't be
from sittin'! It'll be from fightin' to get up and get out!

(She sings)
Some people can get a thrill
Knitting sweaters and sitting still—
    That's okay for some people who don't know they're
    alive;

Some people can thrive and bloom,
Living life in a living room—
    That's perfect for some people of one hundred and five!

But I
At least gotta try,
When I think of all the sights that I gotta see yet,
All the places I gotta play,
All the things that I gotta be yet—
    Come on, Poppa, whaddaya say?

Some people can be content
Playing bingo and paying rent—
    That's peachy for some people,
    For some humdrum people
To be,
But some people ain't me!

I had a dream,
A wonderful dream, Poppa,
    All about June and the Orpheum Circuit—
    Give me a chance and I know I can work it!
I had a dream,
Just as real as can be, Poppa—
There I was in Mr. Orpheum's office
And he was saying to me,
"Rose!
Get yourself some new orchestrations,
New routines and red velvet curtains,

Get a feathered hat for the Baby,
Photographs in front of the theatre,
Get an agent—and in jig time
You'll be being booked in the big time!"
Oh, what a dream,
A wonderful dream, Poppa,
And all that I need
Is eighty-eight bucks, Poppa!
That's what he said, Poppa,
Only eighty-eight bucks, Poppa . . .

POP: You ain't gettin' eighty-eight cents from me, Rose! *(He goes)*

ROSE *(Shouting after him)*: Then I'll get it someplace else—but I'll get it and get my kids out!

(She sings)
Goodbye
To blueberry pie!
Good riddance to all the socials I had to go to,
All the lodges I had to play,
All the Shriners I said hello to—
Hey, L.A., I'm coming your way!
Some people sit on their butts,
Got the dream—yeah, but not the guts!
    That's living for some people,
    For some humdrum people,
I suppose.
    Well, they can stay and rot—

(She starts out, takes the plaque from the wall, dumps it in her purse, then finishes her song)

    But not
Rose!

(And she strides out)

(The lights black out)

Scene Three

A road.

In front of the curtain, June and Louise—wearing their coats and hats and carrying suitcases—stand trying to thumb a ride. The music of "Some People" is continuous underneath. The cut-out of a fancy old touring car "driven" by a rich man and his little son comes on and stops to pick up the children. But as they get in, June signals—and Rose comes running out carrying a suitcase and Chowsie.

She sings as the car "drives" across. Behind it, boys cross carrying signs indicating the lessening distance between Seattle and Rose's goal: Los Angeles.

They pass an urchin tap dancing, his hat held out for money. Rose puts some pennies in his cap, then, impressed by his dancing, she yanks him into the car and they move on.

A troop of boy scouts passes, singing. Rose hears the last little boy hold a good high note—and yanks him into the car.

At last, they reach a welcome banner: LOS ANGELES. *The car stops. Rose gets out with her daughters and the dog and the suitcases and the two stolen boys. The car drives away and as the little band marches off gaily, Rose brings up the rear—with the rich man's tearful little boy, whom she has also stolen.*

Scene Four

The illuminated placards change to read:

The backstage of a vaudeville house. There are odds and ends of scenery, crates, trunks, lights, etc.

Mr. Weber, the theatre manager, rushes on, followed by Rose and her exhausted brood, who collapse near the wings.

WEBER: No, Madam Rose, no!

ROSE: Now listen, Mr. Weber, I did not come all the way from Seattle to Los Angeles to take "No" for an answer.

WEBER: You'll take it from me.

ROSE: Because you don't know how to run your theatre. Your business is slipping. You need youth, fresh young talent.

WEBER: Madam Rose, I told you this morning, I told you this afternoon and I am telling you now: if there is anything I hate worse than kids, it's kids on stage!

ROSE: Children, go play in the alley. *(As they go)* Mr. Weber, that was a rotten remark. If you were a gentleman, you'd apologize and book my act.

WEBER: I am not a gentleman.

(A nice-looking man carrying a suitcase enters. He has a sweetly sad, tired quality)

14

ROSE: Oh, deep down, you are. And if you—

WEBER *(To the man)*: Herbie! I been looking for you to get your opinion of the show.

HERBIE: I doubled your crackerjack order, Ed.

WEBER: That bad?

HERBIE: Except for a coupla acts. I left a memo on your desk.

(A sexual look between Herbie and Rose)

ROSE: Mr. Weber, you left me right in the middle of a sentence.

WEBER: Madam Rose, you're always in the middle of a sentence.

ROSE: But if your show is as bad as this intelligent gentleman says, you could certainly try my act for a few nights. *(To Herbie)* Couldn't he?

HERBIE: Yeah, he could. You could, Ed.

WEBER: What??

HERBIE: Your theatre gets a family audience. They love kids.

ROSE: And my kids are great!

HERBIE: They sure are.

(Rose and Weber gape)

WEBER: How do you know?

HERBIE: I've seen 'em.

WEBER: Where?

HERBIE: In—Seattle. They'd give your show a lift, Ed.

WEBER: Well...

ROSE: Listen—

WEBER: Stop pushing. Let me think it over. *(He goes)*

ROSE: Gee—it's hard for me to say thanks!

HERBIE: You just said it.

ROSE: Why'd he listen to you?

HERBIE: Everybody in show business listens to anybody. Besides, I used to book acts into this theatre.

ROSE: Are you an agent?

HERBIE: I was but I'm in the candy business now: I sell to vaudeville houses all over the West.

ROSE: How could you ever leave show business?

HERBIE: When the acts I handled had too little talent, I got sick to my stomach. Ulcers.

ROSE: You're too sympathetic.

HERBIE: Also I went bust. I was always giving them my commission and telling them they got a raise.

ROSE: The good Lord says charity begins at home.

HERBIE: I don't have a home.

ROSE *(Eyes him)*: You're not married?

HERBIE: I had five sisters, and the ugly one didn't get married until a year ago.

ROSE: . . . Why'd you help me just now?

HERBIE: I love kids.

ROSE: Oh.

HERBIE: Also—I saw you before.

ROSE: Where?

HERBIE: Waiting outside Weber's office. You looked like a pioneer woman without a frontier.

ROSE: I don't suppose you'd consider being an agent again.

HERBIE: Would you consider marrying again?

ROSE: How do you know I'm not married now?

HERBIE: I asked your kids about you.

ROSE: Oh. Well, after three husbands, it takes a lot of butter to get you back in the frying pan.

HERBIE: After twenty years of show business— *(Picks up bag)* —you kinda breathe better in the real world.

ROSE: Funny.

(Music starts)

HERBIE: What?

ROSE: Us. I like you—but I don't want marriage. You like me— but you don't want show business.

HERBIE: That seems to leave you there—and me here.

ROSE: Oh, that depends on how you look at it. You look at what we don't have, I look at what we do have.

(She sings)
Funny, you're a stranger who's come here,
    Come from another town.
Funny, I'm a stranger myself here—
Small world, isn't it?
Funny, you're a man who goes traveling
    Rather than settling down.
Funny, 'cause I'd love to go traveling—
Small world, isn't it?

We have so much in common,
    It's a phenomenon.
We could pool our resources
By joining forces
    From now on.
Lucky, you're a man who likes children—
    That's an important sign.
Lucky, I'm a woman with children—
Small world, isn't it?
Funny, isn't it?
    Small, and funny, and fine.

(Music continues as Weber returns)

WEBER: Well, I'm not gonna pay you much money.

ROSE: Oh, you'll have to talk about money to Herbie.

WEBER: You handling her act?!

HERBIE: Well—no, I—

(Looks at her. She moves suggestively and he laughs)

—yeah, I guess I am.

WEBER *(As he goes)*: I'll be in the office.

ROSE *(Singing happily)*:
>We have so much in common,
>>It's a phenomenon.
>
>We could pool our resources
>By joining forces
>>From now on.

HERBIE: Rose . . . is that act of yours any good?

ROSE: Good? It's great—and June is absolutely sensational! Wait till you see it!

(Singing)
>Lucky, you're a man who likes children—
>>That's an important sign.
>
>Lucky, I'm a woman with children—
>Small world, isn't it?
>Funny, isn't it?
>>Small, and funny, and fine.

(The lights fade out)

Scene Five

The illuminated placards change to read:

BABY JUNE AND HER NEWSBOYS

LOS ANGELES

The curtains part to show a street drop typical of vaudeville; before it, a newspaper kiosk. The orchestra is a tacky, rickety vaudeville combination that tears into the screeching musical introduction for Baby June and Her Newsboys. The Boys, of course, are Louise and the three little kids Rose stole en route to L.A. Their costumes are cheap representations of newsboy outfits, and they wave papers wildly as they sing.

NEWSBOYS *(Singing)*:
> Extra! Extra! Hey, look at the headline!
> Historical news is being made!
> Extra! Extra! They're drawing a red line
> Around the biggest scoop of the decade!
> A barrel of charm, a fabulous thrill!
> The biggest little headline in vaud-e-ville:

(Spoken—to ecstatic drum rolls) Presenting—in person—that three-foot-three bundle of dynamite: BABY JUNE!

(There is the greatest drum roll of them all, and crashing through the "front page" plastered across the kiosk comes June, wearing the gaudiest, fanciest, richest costume Rose has been able to whip

19

up. She whirls madly to the footlights, does a split and coyly screeches—)

JUNE: Hello, everybody! My name is June. What's yours!

(Then, assisted by the Newsboys, June sings a ragtime version of "Let Me Entertain You")

Let me entertain you,
Let me make you smile.
  Let me do a few tricks,
  Some old and then some new tricks—
I'm very versatile!
  And if you're real good,
  I'll make you feel good—
I want your spirits to climb.
So let me entertain you
And we'll have a real good time—yessir!
We'll have a real good time!

(After that, she tap dances wildly about the stage and does every trick Rose has been able to teach, steal and think up. She has a big finish—with the Boys offstage, of course. She squeals as she does high kicks for her bows and then, breathing as though each gasp were her last, she trips daintily to the footlights and says—)

Thank you so much, ladies and gentlemen. You're *very* kind . . . You know, everybody has someone to thank for their success. Usually, it's their mother; sometimes, it's their father. But tonight, I'd like you all to join me in giving thanks to an uncle of mine—and an uncle of yours. The Greatest Uncle of Them All: OUR—UNCLE—SAM!

(A crash from the orchestra and, as June darts behind the kiosk to change her costume, the Newsboys and Louise return—in military costumes. Each of the three Boys represents a wing of our armed forces; Louise is Uncle Sam. Each child does whatever he can for a specialty; Louise does a trick step—which she also did

in the opening. The pièce de résistance *is, naturally, June. This time she is dressed like a red, white and blue Statue of Liberty and she is on point, twirling batons for all she is worth. Behind her, the American eagle pops up over the kiosk; the band plays "The Stars and Stripes." But Rose takes no chances. As June twirls herself into a split, Louise and the Boys fire the rifles they are carrying—and American flags pop up. Wild applause, stopped by June, breathing harder than ever)*

Mr. Conductor, if you please.

(The orchestra strikes up again and June and her Newsboys start a traveling step. As the music builds and gets faster, the name of the city on the illuminated placard changes. It goes from one town to another, finally winding up with AKRON. *During this, however, the lights on the performers begin to flicker faster and faster—and as June and her Boys seem to dance faster and faster, they appear to be flying through space and growing. Actually, through the flickering dissolve they are replaced by another June, another Louise, and other Boys—all in the same costumes as the originals, but all older and bigger. Time has passed. The act is the same, but the cast is older and the placard has changed to read:*

DAINTY JUNE AND HER NEWSBOYS
AKRON

The music ends with a flourish. The older June blows the same coy kiss and squeals with the same high-kick bow that the Baby June did, and—thank heaven—the lights black out)

Scene Six

The placards read:

"HAPPY BIRTHDAY"

AKRON

Two plaster-cracked hotel rooms.

An alarm clock is ringing wildly as the light comes up on the smaller room. It is festooned with clotheslines hung with winter underwear, costumes, etc. On the bare bedsprings of the one bed lies Louise, wrapped up in a blanket of a very distinct pattern. The mattress has been put on the floor and on it, wrapped in another blanket of the same pattern, are three of the boys in the act. Asleep on two chairs pushed together is the oldest, best-looking and brightest boy in the act: Tulsa. He is also wrapped in one of the blankets. There is one small window with the shade down.

As the alarm keeps ringing, Louise reaches out and shuts it off. A moment, then she bolts upright and looks around. Carefully then, she reaches out, sets the alarm off again and lies back quickly.

YONKERS *(From the floor. A wiseguy)*: Awright, awright!

L.A. *(Sweet-ass)*: We're up, Madam Rose!

YONKERS *(Looks at clock)*: Hey, it ain't even ten o'clock! Turn it off!

L.A. Louise!

TULSA *(Quietly)*: Turn it off, Plug.

LOUISE *(Sits up and turns off the alarm. Yawns elaborately)*: Was that the alarm?

YONKERS: No, it was your mother singing! Shut up!

LOUISE: I was having the loveliest dream. About a special day— My dream book says you dream about a day like that because it maybe really is your—

ANGIE: We wanna sleep!

LOUISE: I just wanted to say—

(She catches Tulsa's eye. He shakes his head)

I'm sorry. *(Silence. She watches them return to sleep. Then she gets out of bed with a great clomping. No reaction. She goes to the window and considers the shade, finally yanking it up quickly. It rolls up with a tremendous clatter—but not a drop of light comes in: the window is smack up against a brick wall. She sticks her head out, craning her neck like mad to see the sky)* How can you all sleep on such a beautiful day!!

YONKERS: Easy—if you shut up.

LOUISE: Do you suppose that sun is so bright because—

(June enters from the other room. Her hair is in curlers; she wears a frilly nightgown and robe)

JUNE: You woke up Mother.

LOUISE *(Whispering)*: I didn't mean to, June. But today is . . . well, you know.

JUNE: Today is one day we don't have to travel and we don't have to rehearse.

YONKERS: Which means we could sleep!

LOUISE: Is Momma mad?

JUNE: She's in the bathroom—making coffee. *(To the Boys)* She says as long as *she's* up, everybody come have breakfast.

LOUISE: June—

JUNE: Honest, Louise!

(June goes out as the Boys groan. Louise groans back at them)

LOUISE: I said I was sorry!

(A moment, then she timidly goes into the other room. The light comes up just a trifle as she enters, but the room is very dim. It is much larger than the other room. Louise speaks, wistfully)

Momma? . . . Momma?

ROSE *(Calling)*: Happy birthday!

(The bathroom door bursts open and out comes Rose in a battered bathrobe, carrying a small birthday cake with lighted candles. She, June and the Boys—who pop up and come crashing through the doorway—sing "Happy Birthday" to Louise, who is startled and cries happily. One of the boys turns on the lights and the room is bright and gay. There is a big bed and a table near it. Little dogs run about yapping; there are June's cat, a monkey chained to the bed and bird cages suspended from the chandelier, etc. There are yells of "Surprise! Surprise!" "Blow out the candles," "Make a wish," hugs and kisses, etc.)

Make a wish!

LOUISE: I wish . . . oh, Momma, I wish—

ROSE: Oh! That rotten monkey ate a piece outa the cake! *(Going to the monkey)* Gigolo! Bad, Gigolo, bad bad! *(Then, looking at the blanket Louise has draped over her pajamas)* Say, that would make a good coat.

(Louise blows out the candles)

YONKERS: Hey, there's only ten candles on this cake!

ROSE: What do you care? You ain't gonna eat candles.

YONKERS: But she only had ten candles last year.

L.A.: And the year before that.

YONKERS: Come to think of it, she's had ten candles for the last—

ROSE: STOP RIGHT THERE! As long as we have this act, nobody is over twelve and you all know it! Excepting of course me and—where's Herbie? I had a dream— Tulsa, go across the hall and see what's keeping Herbie. The rest of you can give Louise her presents while I see if the chow mein is warmed up.

YONKERS: Chow mein?

LOUISE: It's my birthday!

YONKERS: But chow mein for breakfast??

ROSE: Why not? There's egg roll, ain't there? *(She exits into the bathroom)*

YONKERS: If Madam Rose paid us a salary, we coulda *bought* you presents, Louise— *(He has picked up a box from under the bed)* But it's more fun to clip from the five and dime anyway. *(Hands her the box proudly)* It's a catcher's mitt and a big-league baseball.

LOUISE: Thank you, Yonkers.

L.A.: Here's a real stuffed cat.

ANGIE: I clipped a bowl of goldfish. But they caught me, so I drew a fish instead.

LOUISE: I love it. Oh, June, what a beautiful package!

JUNE: It's a complete sewing set in a velvet-lined basket.

(They embrace. Tulsa, who has come back into the room, picks up his present—three second-hand books tied with cord—and puts it into Louise's hands)

TULSA: I should have wrapped them.

LOUISE *(Very touched)*: You don't have to wrap books.

TULSA: Well—happy birthday, Plug.

LOUISE: Happy birthday, Tulsa. I mean, you're welcome.

(Rose comes out of the bathroom carrying food. During the following, the others help by arranging the plates and food)

ROSE: All right, one egg roll apiece and no more.

TULSA: Herbie wasn't in his room, Madam Rose.

ROSE *(Stops dead)*: He wasn't?

TULSA: No.

ROSE: Where could he be?

LOUISE: Momma, can I see my present from you, please?

ROSE: It's from Herbie and me.

LOUISE: It's not from Herbie. He's an agent. It's from *you.*

ROSE: Well, I picked it out, but Herbie paid for it—with his commission for a whole month.

YONKERS: Old Herb makes the same salary we do!

ROSE: Inside, you, and get the coffee! *(Serving food)* Here I am, busting to tell Herbie the dream I had—

LOUISE: Momma—

ROSE: It's really in your honor, coming on the very evening of your birthday. *(To June)* Oh, Baby! You'll love it. You all will. It's— *(Looks toward door, then makes a gesture of dismissal)* —children, it's a *new act!*

YONKERS: That ain't a dream, it's a miracle!

ROSE: In this dream, I saw June singing a song in like a barn-yard. And then—a cow came on stage.

TULSA: A cow??

YONKERS: That's pretty sexy.

ROSE: Not a real cow. Sort of a dancing cow—with a great big smile. And that cow—that cow leaned right over my bed and spoke to me!

JUNE *(Cynically)*: What did the cow say?

(A knocking on the door)

KRINGELEIN *(Offstage)*: Madam Rose—

ROSE: I am *not* cooking in here, Mr. Kringelein. That cow—

KRINGELEIN: Open this door!

ROSE: I'm dressing. That cow—

KRINGELEIN: Madam Rose—

ROSE: I'll call you tomorrow when I'm finished. That dear fat cow looked me right in the eye and said: "Rose, if you want to get on the Orpheum Circuit, put *me* in your act." Children, you know what I'm going to do?

YONKERS: You're going to pay that crummy cow and not us!

ROSE: I'm not paying anybody but I am going to take that cow's advice! I'm going to call the new act: Dainty June and Her Farmboys. I'm going to get more boys. I'm going to put that cow in the act—

(Kringelein—a pompous hotel manager—quietly opens the door of the other room, shuts it behind him and tiptoes to the doorway between the two rooms)

—and Chowsie and the monkey. And Louise's present—if you don't mind, honey—

LOUISE: But, Momma, I don't even know what it is!

KRINGELEIN *(Coming into the room. Haughtily)*: No cooking, Madam Rose?

ROSE: How dare you enter a lady's boudoir without knocking?

KRINGELEIN *(Advancing)*: Where's your hot plate?

ROSE: Where's your search warrant?

KRINGELEIN *(Heading toward the bathroom)*: In all the years I have been running a theatrical hotel—

ROSE *(Opening the corridor door)*: If you don't leave, I'm going to scream!

(One of the boys darts to block the bathroom door)

KRINGELEIN *(Pointing toward a sign)*: You know the rules. No cooking. No electrical appliances. No—no pets other than small— *(Pushes the kid out of the way)* —dogs or—

(He opens the bathroom door. A little lamb in rubber drawers runs out between his legs and over to Louise)

ROSE: Happy birthday, darling!

KRINGELEIN: It's a GODDAM ZOO!

ROSE: Profanity in front of my babies! June, get the Bible! Get the Bible!

(People in bathrobes and wrappers begin to appear in the doorway, flowing into the room)

KRINGELEIN: You pack up this dirty menagerie and get out!

ROSE: You'll have to throw me out, you rotten ANIMAL HATER! *(To the others)* That's what he is! Send for the SPCA!

KRINGELEIN: Send for the police! I rented these two rooms to one adult and three children! Now I see one adult! Five pets and one, two, three, four—

ROSE *(Points to one of the boys)*: You counted him twice! *(The kids are running in and out. She turns to the others)* It's a simple little birthday party for my baby—

KRINGELEIN: One, two, three, four—STAND STILL!

ROSE: Chow mein. I'd offer you some but there's only one egg roll—

KRINGELEIN: One, two, three, four, five—how many are sleeping in that room?

ROSE: What room?

KRINGELEIN *(In the doorway between the two rooms)*: THIS room, madam, THIS room!

ROSE *(Pushing him in)*: There isn't a soul in this room. *(Closing the door behind them)* Except you and me. *(She lets out a scream as she shoves him down onto the mattress on the floor)* Mr. Kringelein, what are you trying to do?!! *(Throws pillows and blankets on him)* Mr. Kringelein! Stop! Help! Rape!

(She wrenches her robe open and staggers back into the other room, where the people get a chair for her and ad lib their concern as Rose continues)

My babies! My babies! *MONSTER!* Thank you, Gladys. A little birthday party—chow mein—a tiny little cake—

(Louise, with her lamb, goes into other room during this. Kringelein gets out of the snarl of blankets and exits)

HERBIE'S VOICE *(From the hall)*: Rose! Rose! Are you all right? *(He enters the room and pushes his way to Rose's side)* Rose! What's happened? Are you O.K., honey?

ROSE *(Straightening herself)*: Sure! Where have you— *(Then, re-*

membering) Herbie. Mr. Kringelein, the hotel manager, he—he tried to—to—

HERBIE *(A cynical eye)*: Again? *(He starts for the other room)*

ROSE: Well, I had to do something, Herbie, don't you dare apologize to him!

HERBIE: Where's Louise?

ROSE: A fat lot you care. The child has a birthday—

HERBIE: Does she like her present?

ROSE: I'm surprised you remembered, where've you been? That's what I want to know.

HERBIE *(Bringing forward a mild little man)*: Rose, this is Mr. Goldstone.

ROSE: I ask you, Mr. Goldstone. The child has a birthday once a year. We plan a little party—I'm sorry it's such a small cake and—

HERBIE: Mr. Goldstone is from the Orpheum Circuit.

ROSE: There's only one egg roll and some fried...rice...and sub...gum...chow...

HERBIE: The act is booked on the Orpheum Circuit.

(A long pause. Rose stares, numb with a growing happiness. Mechanically, she picks up a plate from the trunk and holds it out)

ROSE *(Singing)*:
Have an egg roll, Mr. Goldstone,
Have a napkin, have a chopstick, have a chair!
Have a sparerib, Mr. Goldstone—
Any sparerib that I can spare, I'd be glad to share!
Have a dish, have a fork,
Have a fish, have a pork,
Put your feet up, feel at home.
Have a smoke, have a coke,
Would you like to hear a joke?
I'll have June recite a poem!
Have a lichee, Mr. Goldstone,
Tell me any little thing that I can do.

Ginger-peachy, Mr. Goldstone,
Have a kumquat—have two!
Everybody give a cheer—
Santa Claus is sittin' here—
Mr. Goldstone, I love you!

(Hysterical with excitement)

Have a goldstone, Mr. Egg Roll,
Tell me any little thing that I can do.
Have some fried rice, Mr. Soy Sauce,
Have a cookie, have a few!
What's the matter, Mr. G.?
Have another pot of tea!
Mr. Goldstone, I love you!

There are good stones and bad stones
And curbstones and Gladstones
And touchstones and such stones as them!
There are big stones and small stones
And grindstones and gallstones,
But Goldstone is a gem.

There are milestones, there are millstones,
There's a cherry, there's a yellow, there's a blue!
But we don't want any old stone,
Only Goldstone will do!

ALL *(Singing)*:
Moonstone, sunstone—we all scream for one stone!
Mervyn Goldstone, we love you!
Goldstone!

(The lights black out in the larger bedroom and fade in slowly on the small room, where a forgotten Louise sits with the lamb)

LOUISE *(Singing softly)*:
Little lamb, little lamb,
My birthday is here at last.

Little lamb, little lamb,
A birthday goes by so fast.
Little bear, little bear,
You sit on my right, right there.
Little hen, little hen,
What game shall we play, and when?
Little cat, little cat,
Ah, why do you look so blue?
Did somebody paint you like that,
Or is it your birthday, too?
Little fish, little fish,
Do you think I'll get my wish?
Little lamb, little lamb,
I wonder how old I am.
I wonder how old I am . . .

(The lights dim out)

Scene Seven

The placards change to read:

The scene is a section of a gaudy Chinese restaurant. Herbie sits at a table with June. Rose is scraping leftovers from the plates into cartons which she eventually gathers into a paper sack. She hums happily.

ROSE: Hand me Louise's plate, June.

JUNE *(Embarrassed)*: Mother—

ROSE: We're paying for it, ain't we? You'll get an ulcer like Herbie. Besides, what the dogs don't eat, we will.

HERBIE: Rose, did it ever occur to you there might be some-body in this world who *doesn't* like Chinese food?

ROSE: Don't be silly. Who? *(Hums, scrapes; then softly)* Don't you like it, Herbie?

HERBIE *(A beat, then he smiles)*: Sure Rose. I love it.

(Louise enters wearing a coat made of the hotel blanket and holding a little dog that is also wearing a blanket-coat)

ROSE: Did she?

LOUISE: Yes.

ROSE *(Baby talk to the dog)*: 'Atsa healthy-wealthy lady-wadie.

HERBIE: Oh, God!

32

JUNE: Herbie's angry: he's chain smoking.

ROSE: Herbie's never angry, it's bad for his stomach. Come on, girls, beddie-bye.

(She and June put on their blanket-coats)

JUNE: It's so early!

ROSE: You're going to audition for Mr. T. T. Grantziger and his Palace Theatre tomorrow and you have to look *young*.

LOUISE: Can I wear a dress?

ROSE: You'd look old in a dress. Besides, you haven't got one.

JUNE: Good night, Uncle Herbie. *(She kisses him)*

HERBIE: Good night, June. *(Stands up to kiss Louise, who stiff-arms him)* Good night, Louise.

LOUISE: Good night, Herbie. *(She exits with June)*

ROSE: I'll cold-cream their faces and be right back.

HERBIE: The hotel is two doors away! Honestly, you behave as though those girls—Rose!

(This because she is collecting silverware and is about to put it in her bag)

ROSE: We need new silverware. *(Stops, then puts down the silver)* Herbie, how long is it going to take you to get used to me?

HERBIE: How long did it take me to get used to those coats?

ROSE: What's the matter with them? They're real stylish! Louise is very talented with a needle. Herbie, as the good Lord says: an eye for an eye, a tooth for a tooth— *(On this, she sweeps the silver into her bag)* And it serves them right for overcharging.

(Starts to go. Herbie hands her a knife, which she also takes, but she stops and returns)

They can skip the cold cream *for one night.*

(Automatically, he gets up and helps her off with her coat. Rose, admiringly:)

All this time we've been together, and you still stand up for me!

HERBIE: It's instead of standing up *to* you.

ROSE: O.K., you say we're never alone. I wanted to have dinner tonight, just the two of us, but what was I going to do with the girls? They're babies.

HERBIE: Rose, no matter how you dress 'em, no matter how you smother 'em, they're big girls. They're almost young women—

ROSE: They're not and they never will be!

HERBIE: I'm embarrassed in front of them! When are you going to marry me, Rose?

ROSE: Don't forget to take our scrapbooks to Mr. Grantziger's tomorrow.

HERBIE: When are you going to quit stalling? Honey, don't you know there's a depression?

ROSE: Of course I know! I read *Variety*.

HERBIE: Don't you know what it's doing to vaudeville? Don't you know what the talkies are doing to vaudeville? Don't you know I love you?

ROSE: You think I'd be unfaithful to my husbands if you didn't? But I have to think of my girls and their happiness.

HERBIE: Louise is very happy being the front end of a cow!

ROSE: It's better than being the rear end! Anyway, she loves animals.

HERBIE: She and June should both be in school—

ROSE: And be just like other girls; cook and clean and sit and die! (*To a passing waitress, sweetly*) Honey, could I have a spoon to stir my tea? . . . Herbie, I promised June I'd make her a star and I will. I promised I'd get her on the Pantages Circuit and I did. I promised I'd get her on the Orpheum Circuit and I did.

HERBIE: *I* did! And you promised me that after I did, you'd marry me.

ROSE: I promised her she'd headline on Broadway and—

HERBIE: Didn't you hear what I said?

ROSE: Yes, but I'm ignoring it. *(To the waitress, for the spoon)* Thanks, honey. Herbie, it isn't very polite for a gentleman to remind a lady that she welched. There was no date on that promise—

HERBIE: ROSE, STOP HANDING ME—

ROSE: Your stomach! *(Quickly handing him a pill)* Herbie, why don't you get angry outside, instead of letting it settle in your stomach?

HERBIE: I'm afraid.

ROSE: Of me?

HERBIE: Of me.

ROSE: What do you mean?

HERBIE: If I ever let loose, it'll end with me picking up and walking.

ROSE: Only around the block.

HERBIE: No.

ROSE: Don't say that.

> *(Sings)*
> You'll never get away from me.
> You can climb the tallest tree,
>   I'll be there somehow.
> True, you could say, "Hey, here's your hat,"
> But a little thing like that
>   Couldn't stop me now.
> I couldn't get away from you
> Even if you told me to,
>   So go on and try!
> Just try,
> And you're gonna see
> How you're gonna not at all get away from me!

HERBIE: What is it? What do you want? There are better agents.

ROSE: Not for me.

HERBIE: And even weaker men.

ROSE: Not for me.

HERBIE: Then what?

ROSE: You. Oh, Herbie, just help me like you been helping. Just let me get June's name up in lights so big, they'll last my whole life.

HERBIE: Rose, what you expect—

ROSE: I'll *get!* And after I get it, I promise I'll marry you.

(Herbie moves away from the table)

I even promise to keep my promise. *(Silence)* Please, Herbie. I don't want to upset anything before the audition tomorrow. Including your stomach.

HERBIE *(Singing)*:
Rose, I love you,
But don't count your chickens.

ROSE *(Singing)*:
Come dance with me.

HERBIE:
I warn you
That I'm no Boy Scout.

ROSE:
Relax a while—come dance with me.

HERBIE:
So don't think
That I'm easy pickin's—

ROSE:
The music's so nice—

HERBIE:
Rose!
'Cause I just may

Some day
Pick up and pack out.

ROSE:

Oh no, you won't,
No, not a chance.
No arguments,
Shut up and dance.

BOTH:

You'll never get away from me,
You can climb the tallest tree—
I'll be there somehow!

True, you could say "Hey, here's your hat,"
But a little thing like that
Couldn't stop me now.

I couldn't get away from you
Even if I wanted to—

ROSE:

Well, go on and try!
Just try—

HERBIE:

Ah, Rose—

ROSE:

And you're gonna see—

HERBIE:

Ah, Rose—

ROSE:

How you're gonna not at all
Get away from me!

(The lights fade)

Scene Eight

The placards change to read:

GRANTZIGER'S PALACE

NEW YORK

The scene is the stage of a good theatre.

A telephone is ringing as the lights come up on the gold theatre curtains. An attractive, smartly groomed secretary—Cratchitt— hurries on, signals toward the top of the theatre, pulls out a telephone attached on a bracket to the proscenium and answers.

CRATCHITT: Yes, Mr. Grantziger . . . I know, but they're having a little difficulty with their scenery. Well, wait till you see it . . .

(Rose appears wearing a hat and coat)

ROSE *(To the Conductor)* Now keep the tempo bright. Keep it up.

CRATCHITT *(On phone)*: That's the mother . . . I *have* told her!

ROSE *(Peering out front)*: Hello, Mr. Grantziger. Where is he?

CRATCHITT *(Pointing)*: In his office at the top of the theatre.

ROSE *(Waving—neighborly)*: Hi!

HERBIE *(Runs on to try to get Rose off)*: It's a privilege to audition for you, Mr. Grantziger!

ROSE *(Just before Herbie drags her off)*: You're going to love us!

38

(They exit)

CRATCHITT *(Into the phone)*: That's the agent. *He's* nice.

HERBIE *(Returning)*: We're ready now.

CRATCHITT *(Into the phone)*: They're ready now, Mr. Grant-ziger. *(To Herbie)* Good luck.

HERBIE: Thank you.

(They both go off, the lights dim and the curtains part to reveal a corny set of a vaudeville barnyard, complete with haystack. Rose's Newsboys are now Farmboys, and they stand with rakes, hoes, etc., in a picturesque tableau (!) as birds and music twitter the approach of dawn—which comes up violently. The music crashes into the introduction for the Newsboys' song—sung, this time, by the Farmboys—and on cue, the haystack parts for Dainty June to whirl out and down front, where she ends in that same split. This time, she sings and dances with a COW, however. During the dance, the front end of the COW does a familiar trick step: Louise is still doing her big specialty)

FARMBOYS *(Singing)*:
Extra! Extra! Hey look at the headline!
Historical news is being made!
Extra! Extra! They're drawing a red line
Around the biggest scoop of the decade!
A barrel of charm, a fabulous thrill!
The biggest little headline in vaud-e-ville!

(Spoken) Presenting—in person—that five-foot-two bundle of dynamite: DAINTY JUNE!

JUNE: Hello, everybody! My name is June. What's yours?

(She sings)
I have a moo cow, a new cow, a true cow
Named Caroline.

COW: Moo moo moo moo—

JUNE:

    She's an extra special friend of mine.

COW: Moo moo moo moo—

JUNE:

    I like everything about her fine.

COW: Moo moo moo moo—

JUNE:

    She likes to moo in the moonlight
        When the moody moon appears.
    And when she moos in the moonlight,
        Gosh, it's moosic to my ears!
        She's so moosical . . .
    She loves a man cow, a tan cow who can cow
        Her with a glance.

(The Cow recites, "Moo moo moo moo," following this and the next two lines)

    When he winks at her, she starts to dance,
    It's what grownups call a real romance,
    But if we moved to the city
        Or we settled by the shore,
    She'd make the moooooooooove,
        'Cause she loves me more!

(June and the Cow continue the dance to the end and exit. The phone rings. Cratchitt comes on to answer)

CRATCHITT *(Into the phone)*: Yes, Mr. Grantziger. Dainty June, will you come out please?

(June comes on)

Face front, dear. Profile.

(Rose appears in the other wing)

Yes, Mr. Grantziger. Thank you. That's all.

ROSE: But we have a great dramatic finale!

CRATCHITT: I'm sure. But he's seen quite enough.

ROSE: Ahh— *(To the Conductor)* Hit it!

CRATCHITT: But Mr. Grantziger does not want to see any—

(But even while she is talking, the music crashes in and the Farmboys—directed by Rose—dance on in Eton suits with high hats and canes, frightening Cratchitt off. They launch into the song and tap dance that always built up to the entrance of the blond star. And it does this time, for June comes on, dazzling, glamorous, singing and dancing for all she—and Rose—are worth. During the Boys' number, one of the high hats falls off, and Rose dashes out from the wings to retrieve and replace it. At the end of June's song-and-dance with the Boys, Rose helps the stagehands get the haystack offstage. Behind it is the front of a train which puffs smoke)

FARMBOYS *(Singing):*
Broadway, Broadway! We've missed it so!
We're going soon and taking June
To star her in a show!
Bright lights! White lights!
Rhythm and romance!
The train is late so while we wait
We're gonna do a little dance!

(And they do—as a prelude to June's song)

JUNE *(Singing):*
Broadway! Broadway! How great you are!
I'll leave the farm with all its charm
To be a Broadway star!
Bright lights! White lights!
Where the neons glow!
My bag is packed, I've got my act.
So all aboard, come on, let's go!

YONKERS *(Calls):* All aboard!

ROSE: Woo woo . . . Watch this! It's a train.

FARMBOYS: Let's go!

(Waving and "goodbyes" from everybody. A train effect; the Cow tries to run after the train)

JUNE *(To the Cow):* Goodbye, Caroline. I'll write to you.

COW: Moo!

JUNE: Goodbye, Caroline—take care. Don't forget to write! . . . Wait! Stop the train! *(A chord)* Stop everything! I can't go to Broadway with you!

TULSA: Why not, Dainty June?

JUNE *(To soupy music):* Because everything in life that really matters is right here! What care I for tinsel and glamour when I have friendship and true love? I'm staying here with Caroline!

(She runs off the train platform and embraces the Cow to general cheering. A chord from the orchestra—which launches once again into "The Stars and Stripes"; this time the American Eagle— and a big one—pops up over the train; June grabs batons from the platform and twirls them madly as she marches downstage to end in a triumphant split while the Farmboys fire American flags from their canes. Rose has done it again. The light changes to work light and the phone is ringing loudly. Cratchitt comes out to answer it. Rose and Herbie come out from the opposite wing to hear the verdict)

CRATCHITT: Yes, Mr. Grantziger . . . What?? *(To Rose and Herbie, in astonishment)* He liked it! *(On the phone again)* Yes, sir. Yes, sir, if that's want you want. *(Hangs up and turns to Rose)* If you and your tribe will come up to the office—I'll make out the contracts.

(She shoots a peculiar look up to Mr. Grantziger's office and exits as Rose shouts up)

ROSE: You won't be sorry, Mr. Grantziger! *(Herbie yanks her off, but she is right back to add)* This is gonna make ya!

(The lights black out)

Scene Nine

An ornately Gothic office with a door center. Louise and June are seated on a bench. Cratchitt is at a desk, answering the phone.

CRATCHITT: Yes?...No. Mr. Grantziger's busy. He's gone down to the stage. *(Hangs up)* Your mother and her friend are just reading over the contract. They won't be much longer. She's gotta eat *some*time...Say, woman to woman, how old are you?

JUNE: Nine.

CRATCHITT: Nine *what?*

JUNE: Nine going on ten.

CRATCHITT: How long has that been going on?

(Herbie comes in carrying a contract, followed by Rose)

HERBIE: Miss Cratchitt, I think Mr. Grantziger made a mistake in this contract.

CRATCHITT *(Gaily)*: So do I.

(The phone rings. Cratchitt picks it up)

Yes?

ROSE: Happy, girls?

LOUISE: Yes, Momma.

CRATCHITT: No. *(She hangs up)*

HERBIE: Miss Cratchitt, we were auditioning for Grantziger's Palace. This contract is for Grantziger's Variety.

CRATCHITT: That's right.

HERBIE: But the Variety is way down on Twelfth Street.

CRATCHITT: He'll give you a visa to get there.

(The phone rings again)

Yes?

HERBIE: I'd like to talk to Mr. Grantziger.

CRATCHITT *(Hangs up quickly)*: No. Listen, I told you: He's down on the stage.

HERBIE *(Going toward the second door)*: This the way?

CRATCHITT: You can't disturb him. He's still holding auditions.

HERBIE: Then I'll wait.

CRATCHITT: Look, friend. Strictly between us, if I were you I'd sign that contract. There's only one item in that act of yours that the Boss likes: Dainty Little June. He thinks she can be an actress.

ROSE *(As June stands up)*: He's right.

CRATCHITT: Can be—*if.*

HERBIE: If what?

CRATCHITT: If she goes to school for a solid year and takes lessons. He's ready to pay for everything—on one condition. *(To Rose)* You stay away.

ROSE: Stay away? I'm her mother!

CRATCHITT: You said it, I didn't.

HERBIE: What about the act?

CRATCHITT *(Shrugs)*: One week at the Variety.

ROSE: But June *is* the act! How is it supposed to go on without her?

HERBIE: Rose, we could—

ROSE *(To Cratchitt)*: How are Louise and I supposed to live?

CRATCHITT: You might get a job, dear.

ROSE: I have a job, dear, and I do it damn well! My daughters are my job and I have two of them!

LOUISE: Momma, if June—

ROSE: June is my baby! I'm her mother!

(The phone rings)

CRATCHITT *(Answering)*: Yes—

ROSE *Taking it away and slamming the receiver down on the table)*: Don't you dare answer the phone when I'm yelling at you! Nobody knows June like I do and nobody can do for her what I can!

JUNE: Momma, this is my chance to be an actress. Mr. Grantziger can make me a star!

ROSE: You *are* a star! And I made you one! Who's got clippings like she has? Books full of 'em! She don't need lessons any more than she needs Mr. T. T. Grantziger!

CRATCHITT: There isn't a person in show business who doesn't need Mr. Grantziger!

ROSE: Take a good look at *this* person!

HERBIE: Rose—

ROSE: They're so smart in New York!

CRATCHITT: New York is the center of everything.

ROSE: New York is the center of New York! There's a whole country full of people who *know* people!—who know what a mother means to her daughter! It's hicks like you who don't know! And you want to know something else? Grantziger's a hick! He'll get no place!

HERBIE: Rose—

ROSE: He's trying to take my baby away from me, that's what he's trying to do! Well, over my dead body, he will!

(And she storms out the door to the "stage," with Herbie and Cratchitt calling and running out after her. A pause, then Louise picks up the phone left off the hook)

LOUISE *(Quietly)*: No. *(Hangs up)* Momma's just talking big, June. She won't really—

JUNE: Yes, she will.

LOUISE: Maybe Mr. Grantziger will—

JUNE: No, he won't . . . Well, that's show business.

LOUISE: Aren't you happy someone like Mr. T. T. Grantziger thinks you can be a star?

JUNE: You're funny.

LOUISE: Why?

JUNE: You're never jealous.

LOUISE: Oh. Well, I don't have any talent. I don't really mind— except Momma would like it better if I did.

JUNE: I guess that's what she likes about me. Momma's no fool. I'm not a star.

LOUISE: You are.

JUNE: *I'm not!* Mr. Grantziger could make me one.

LOUISE: Momma can make you a star, too.

JUNE *(Ice)*: Momma can do one thing: She can make herself believe anything she makes up. Like with that rhinestone finale dress *you* sewed for me. Momma wants publicity so she makes up a story that three nuns went blind sewing it! Now she believes it. She even believes the act is good.

LOUISE: Isn't it?

JUNE *(Cold anger)*: It's a terrible act and I hate it. I've hated it from the beginning and I hate it more now. I hate pretending I'm two years old. I hate singing those same awful songs, doing those same awful dances, wearing those same awful costumes— I didn't mean it about the costumes.

LOUISE: No. You just meant you're too big for them now.

JUNE: . . . Do you ever feel like you didn't have a sister?

LOUISE: . . . Sometimes.

JUNE: It's Momma's fault.

LOUISE: You can't blame everything on Momma.

JUNE: *You* can't maybe. I wish she'd marry Herbie and let me alone.

LOUISE: Herbie doesn't want to marry her. All he cares about is the act.

47

JUNE: Honest, Louise.

LOUISE: Well, he's an agent!

HERBIE *(Enters and tosses the contract back on the desk)*: Your mother isn't feeling well. I'm going to take her back to the hotel . . . Don't worry, I'll get you a good booking. *(He kisses June, looks at Louise who looks away and exits)*

LOUISE: I wish Momma would marry a plain man . . . so we'd all be together.

(She sings)
If Momma was married we'd live in a house,
As private as private can be:
Just Momma, three ducks, five canaries, a mouse,
Two monkeys, one father, six turtles and me . . .
If Momma was married.

JUNE *(Singing)*:
If Momma was married, I'd jump in the air
And give all my toeshoes to you.
I'd get all these hair ribbons out of my hair,
And once and for all, I'd get Momma out, too . . .
If Momma was married.

LOUISE:
Momma, get out your white dress!
You've done it before—

JUNE:
Without much success—

BOTH:
Momma, God speed and God bless,
We're not keeping score—
What's one more or less?
Oh, Momma, say yes
And waltz down the aisle while you may.

LOUISE:

> I'll gladly support you,
> I'll even escort you—

JUNE:

> And I'll gladly give you away!

BOTH:

> Oh, Momma, get married today!

JUNE:

> If Momma was married there wouldn't be any more—
> "Let me entertain you,
> Let me make you smile.
> I will do some kicks."

LOUISE:

> "I will do some tricks."

JUNE:

> Sing out, Louise!

LOUISE:

> Smile, baby!
> Momma, please take our advice:
> We aren't the Lunts.

JUNE:

> I'm not Fanny Brice.
> Momma, we'll buy you the rice,
> If only this once

BOTH:

> You wouldn't think twice!
> It could be so nice
> If Momma got married to stay.

LOUISE:

But Momma gets married—

JUNE:

And—

LOUISE:

Married—

JUNE:

And—

LOUISE:

Married

BOTH:

And never gets carried away.
Oh, Momma,
Oh, Momma,
Oh, Momma, get married today!

(The lights dim out)

Scene Ten

The placards change to read:

"DREAMS OF GLORY"

BUFFALO

A theatre alley, with steps that lead up to the stage door.

Without music, Tulsa is dancing, rehearsing a routine with a broom for a partner. Herbie comes out the stage door and watches until Tulsa sees him and stops in embarrassment.

HERBIE: That's pretty fancy footwork, Tulsa. Why don't you show it to Madam Rose?

TULSA: I'm not that good, Herbie. It's just foolin' around.

HERBIE *(As, unseen by him, Louise enters)*: You started "foolin' around" about three months ago. Just after Mr. Grantziger canceled our booking.

TULSA: Well...

HERBIE: Why, Tulsa?

LOUISE: He's just had more time, that's all. Like that two-week layoff in Albany.

TULSA: And the layoff in Rochester.

LOUISE: And the layoff in Niagara Falls.

HERBIE: Oh. I thought you were maybe worried about the act.

TULSA: Oh, no, Herbie.

HERBIE: Because the way things are pickin' up—why, I

51

wouldn't be surprised if you kids got paid! *(To Louise)* Matter of fact, they're good enough right now for me to treat you to an icecream soda.

LOUISE: No, thank you.

HERBIE: Chow mein?

LOUISE: Momma doesn't like us to eat just before a show.

HERBIE *(After a moment, strong)*: Louise—there's one thing your momma knows that I wish you did: I like her. *(He starts toward the stage door)*

LOUISE: Herbie...*(He stops. A moment, then she shakes her head)* Nothing.

HERBIE: Tulsa, if you or any of the boys have any problems, you bring 'em to me.

TULSA: Sure, Herbie.

(Herbie exits)

LOUISE: You didn't tell him, did you? I mean that you're rehearsing a dance-team act?

TULSA: How'd you know I was?

LOUISE: I saw you practicing Monday after the matinée, with your broom for a partner. I was up in the flies.

TULSA: Louise—

LOUISE: Oh, I won't tell anybody, Tulsa! I'm very secretive. Just like you. *(Takes his hand)* See? That's what this means in your palm. And this means you make up dreams—just like me.

TULSA: What do you make up dreams about, Louise?

LOUISE: ...People.

TULSA: Oh, I do that too.

LOUISE: Yes, but yours are about a partner for your act.

TULSA: She's gonna be more than a partner, I hope. I mean I dream...well, you know...*(He starts to dance around)*

LOUISE: What would she have to be like, Tulsa? A wonderful singer and dancer, I guess.

TULSA: No. I'm going to do most of that. I don't mean I'm going to hog it but—they always look at the girl . . . in a dance team. Especially if she's pretty.

LOUISE: Makeup can help. And costumes.

TULSA: I've got the costumes all figured out. A blue satin tux for me—

LOUISE: With rhinestone lapels—

TULSA: You think?

LOUISE: I'll sew them on.

(Music)

TULSA *(As the music starts)*: O.K. Thanks. Well, I pretend I'm home getting ready for a date. I'm combing my hair. I take a flower. Put it in my lapel. Then I spot the audience.

(He sings)
Once my clothes were shabby,
Tailors called me "Cabbie,"
So I took a vow,
  Said "This bum'll
  Be Beau Brummel."
Now I'm smooth and snappy,
Now my tailor's happy.
  I'm the cat's meow,
  My wardrobe is a wow:
Paris silk, Harris tweed,
There's only one thing I need.
Got my tweed pressed,
Got my best vest,
  All I need now is the girl!
Got my striped tie,
Got my hopes high,
  Got the time and the place, and I got rhythm—
  Now all I need's the girl to go with 'em!
If she'll
Just appear, we'll
  Take this big town for a whirl,

53

And if she'll say, "My
Darling, I'm yours," I'll throw away my
   Striped tie and my best-pressed tweed—
   All I really need
   Is the girl!

(Louise has been watching with yearning and now, as Tulsa begins to dance, the yearning increases. He explains his dance to her as he goes along)

I start easy . . . Now I'm more—debonair . . . Break! And I sell it here . . . I start this step—double it—and she appears! All in white!

(He reaches out his hand to the invisible partner, and Louise—who has gotten up—holds out her hand, tentatively. He is unaware of her, unaware of her hopes, unaware she is following him about, visualizing herself as the partner for him)

I take her hand—kiss it—and lead her out on the floor . . . This step is good for the costumes . . . Now we waltz. Strings come in. And I lift her! . . . Again! . . . Once more! . . . Now the tempo changes; all the lights come up; and I build for the finale!

(At last, he starts a step that Louise knows, and, clumsily, she starts to do it with him. At last, he notices and shouts)

That's it, Louise! But do it over here! Give me your hand! Faster! Now Charleston right! Again! Again! Turn!

(She is dancing joyously, her happiness making up for her awkwardness. They end together—in triumph. L.A. runs in from the stage door in costume for the Cow Act and whistles to them. They get up and race into the theatre)

(The lights dim out)

Scene Eleven

The placards change to read:

"TERMINAL"

OMAHA

The scene is a railroad platform. It is a misty night. Baggage is piled near Rose and Herbie. Yonkers and Angie are there.

ROSE: Don't lower yourself to argue, Herbie. If those rats want to quit the act, let them quit. If they want their train tickets home, give them their bus tickets home. *(Crossing)* What's keeping those girls?

HERBIE: There's plenty of time, Rose.

ROSE *(Going to the end of the platform, peering out)*: And you say they're big enough to take care of themselves.

HERBIE: Look, fellas, I know we've had a couple of layoffs in the—

YONKERS: It ain't that, Herbie.

HERBIE: Then what is it?

YONKERS: We're—too old.

HERBIE *(Sotto voce)*: Would you be too old if Madam Rose and I could see our way clear to increasing your salary?

ROSE *(A bellow from clear across the stage)*: Increase what salary?!

ANGIE: Herbie's been paying us—

YONKERS *(Kicks him)*: Moron!

ROSE *(Coming back)*: Herbie . . .

HERBIE: How long is it going to take you to get used to me, Rose?

ROSE: Button your coat. *(To the Boys)* Ingrates! You take the bread out of that man's mouth and spit it in his face! Well, as the good Lord says, "Good riddance to bad rubbish." Give 'em their tickets, Herbie. They were both rotten in the act anyway.

HERBIE: O.K. *(He takes out tickets as she peers out for the girls)*

YONKERS: Thanks, Herbie. Only we'd like tickets for all the fellows.

HERBIE: . . . All the fellows?

YONKERS: Well, they asked us.

HERBIE: You're all leaving?

ANGIE: Yes, sir, Herbie.

ROSE: Something's funny. Something's very funny here.

HERBIE: Why, Angie? *(Silence)*

ROSE: What's this all about? *(Silence)*

HERBIE: O.K. If you're all going, you're all going. But why, Yonkers—

(Louise runs on, a note in her hand)

ROSE: Where've you been? Where's June? *(Silence)* Louise, where's June?

(Louise holds out the note)

Don't give me any of your poems to read now. Answer me!

LOUISE: June wrote this. To you.

ROSE: Wrote what? What's she writing me for?

LOUISE: Momma, *read it!*

(Rose looks at her, then takes the letter. She reads it, then sits and stares at it, not moving, looking like a dead woman through the following)

ANGIE *(To Herbie)*: She eloped.

YONKERS: She didn't elope, stupid. They got married three weeks ago.

HERBIE: Who got married?

YONKERS: June and Tulsa. Only they hadda wait till their act was ready before they took off.

ANGIE: It's a keen act. Ain't it, Louise?

LOUISE: I didn't see it.

YONKERS: We ain't rats, Herbie. We just knew that without June—

HERBIE: Where'd they go?

ANGIE: Well, first they got a club date in Kansas City...

YONKERS *(Kicks him)*: Big mouth! Could we have the tickets now, please, Herbie? We gotta get moving. See, we fixed up an act of our own and—

HERBIE: Get moving!

L.A.: Don't be sore, Herbie. Geez, it ain't our fault the act's washed up.

(He and Angie start off)

HERBIE: Hey, fellas. Good Luck!

YONKERS *(Brightens)*: Thanks. Good luck to you, Herbie.

ANGIE: Good luck, Louise.

LOUISE: Good luck.

YONKERS: Good luck, Madam Rose. *(Silence)* Come on, Angie.

(They go off. Louise stands a good distance from Rose, who has not moved. Herbie goes to Rose and speaks with growing passion)

HERBIE: Rose...Honey, listen. I can go back in the candy business. It's steady: fifty-two weeks all year every year. I'll work my fingers to the bone; I'll do twice what I did before and that was pretty fair. Rose, I could be a district manager and we could stay put in one place. We could have our own house. Louise could go to school. Rose?

Rose, honey, you still got Herbie. You can marry me and I promise you, you won't have one single worry the rest of your life. Rose, don't you want that?

LOUISE *(A burst)*: Yes! *Momma, say yes!*

(Herbie turns and looks at her. A moment, then she runs across the platform into his arms. He holds her tight and rocks her)

Herbie . . .

HERBIE: You read palms, I read minds. It's O.K. *(Going back to Rose, brighter)* It's going to be fine now, honey. Everything happens for the best. O.K., the act's finished. But you and me and our daughter, we're going to have a home—say, we got a cow for the backyard! Why, we are going to be the best damn—

(During the last, Rose slowly gets up and brushes Herbie aside as though she has not heard a word. The letter hangs from her hand as she walks—as though in a trance—to Louise. Her voice is flat and deadly calm)

ROSE: I'm used to people walking out. When my own mother did it, I cried for a week. Your father did it, and then the man I married after him did it, and now— *(Unaware, she tears the letter in half)* Well this time, I'm not crying. This time, I'm apologizing. To you. I pushed you aside for her. I made everything only for her.

LOUISE: No, Momma.

ROSE: But she says I can't make her an actress like she wants to be. The boys walk because they think the act's finished. They think we're nothing without her. *(Now going over the edge)* Well, she's nothing without me! *(Throws the pieces of the letter in the air)* I'm her mother and I made her! And I can make you now! And I will, my baby, I swear I will! I'm going to *make* you a star! I'm going to build a whole new act—all around you! It's going to be better than anything we ever did before! Better than anything we even dreamed!

HERBIE: Rose!

ROSE *(An express train out of control)*: You're right, Herbie! It *is* for the best! The old act was getting stale and tired! But the new one?! Look at the new star, Herbie! She's going to be beautiful! She *is* beautiful! Finished?! We're just beginning and there's no stopping us this time!

I had a dream,
A dream about you, Baby!
It's gonna come true, Baby!
They think that we're through,
But,
Baby,
You'll be swell, you'll be great,
Gonna have the whole world on a plate!
Starting here, starting now,
   Honey, everything's coming up roses!
Clear the decks, clear the tracks,
You got nothing to do but relax
Blow a kiss, take a bow—
   Honey, everything's coming up roses!
Now's your inning—
   Stand the world on its ear!
Set it spinning,
'N that'll be just the beginning!
Curtain up, light the lights,
You got nothing to hit but the heights!
You'll be swell,
   You'll be great,
I can tell—
   Just you wait!
That lucky star I talk about is due!
Honey, everything's coming up roses for me and for you!

You can do it,
   All you need is a hand.

We can do it,
Momma is gonna see to it!

(Herbie and Louise stand silent, numb, as she plows on, singing triumphantly)

Curtain up, light the lights,
We got nothing to hit but the heights!
I can tell,
   Wait and see!
There's the bell,
   Follow me,
And nothing's gonna stop us till we're through!
Honey, everything's coming up roses and daffodils,
Everything's coming up sunshine and Santa Claus,
Everything's gonna be bright lights and lollipops,
Everything's coming up roses for me and for you!

(The curtain falls)

ACT TWO

Scene One

Before the curtain, the illuminated placards read:

MME. ROSE'S TOREADORABLES
TEXAS

It is desert country. Late afternoon. The rear end of a touring car sticks out from one side. From the other, part of a tent.

ROSE *(Calling)*: Are you ready, Louise?

LOUISE *(Off)*: Yes, Momma.

ROSE: Ready, girls?

GIRLS *(Off)*: Yes, Madam Rose.

ROSE: Now don't let the past discourage you. Remember: you're artists of the theatre! *(She imitates a trumpet call)* Madam Rose's Toreadorables!

(A crash of Spanish-type music and an assortment of Girls lurches on in ghastly, homemade señorita costumes. What they lack in talent—everything—they make up for in enthusiasm. And what do they sing? The same opening as the Newsboys and Farmboys, their predecessors)

GIRLS *(As Rose yells for them to "Sing out!")*:
Extra! Extra! Hey, look at the headline!
Historical news is being made!
Extra! Extra! They're drawing a red line

Around the biggest scoop of the decade!
A barrel of charm, a fabulous thrill!
The biggest little headline in vaud-e-ville!

ROSE: Now sell it! Sell it! And give it atmosphere!

GIRLS: Presenting—in person—that five-foot-four bundle of dynamite: SEÑORITA LOUISE!

ROSE: Come on, Louise, come on!

(Louise comes on in a glittering, gaudy toreador costume—and a blond wig. She makes a pathetic attempt to twirl and do a split like June before saying—)

LOUISE: Olé, everybody! My name's Louise. What's yours?
(She looks up at Rose in appeal. A pause. Then—)

ROSE: Well—it's coming along.

LOUISE: Momma, I'm just no good at it.

ROSE: Don't be silly. Let's try the finale. If you have a good strong finish, they'll forgive anything!

(The Cow runs on)

You're late . . . Now, girls, make it stirring!

(She again imitates a trumpet call—and the music launches into—surprise—"The Stars and Stripes." Louise tries vainly to twirl that same baton)

Pick your feet up, Louise, pick 'em up!

(Herbie strolls on wearily in time for the finale: the Girls remove their Spanish shawls and turn them around to form an American flag. But the stars are on bottom, there is much switching and when the last note is ended, the stars are in place but some of the stripes go the wrong way. Rose looks at Herbie's face)

They're tired. Up to your tent, girls. Get ready for bed.

AGNES *(One of the girls)*: Good night, Madam Rose.

ROSE: Good night, Louise. *(Rose takes the blond wig from Louise and kisses her good night. Then she calls to the others)* Don't forget to write your mothers. For money! *(To Herbie)* How'd you make out in town?

HERBIE: Not even a lodge hall.

ROSE: They're too damn un-American down here, that's the trouble. *(Starts to brush the wig)* We better talk about heading up north after I tell the girls their bedtime story.

HERBIE: Once upon a time, there was a prince named Ziegfeld—

ROSE: It could happen!...Anyway, everybody needs something impossible to hope for.

HERBIE: Rose...Why do you make Louise wear that wig in the act?

ROSE: It makes her look more like—a star.

HERBIE: And why do you keep that cow?

ROSE: Herbie, if that cow goes, I go! *(As Louise enters behind them in pajamas)* The act can be fixed. If I was doing it for June, I'd have it all set.

LOUISE: But you're not, and I'm not June.

HERBIE: Now, Plug, nobody expects you to—

LOUISE *(Quietly)*: Herbie, I love you very much but you always let everything slide.

ROSE: He does not!

LOUISE *(Quietly)*: Momma, I love you so much I've tried hard as I could. The act is rotten and I'm rotten in it.

ROSE: How do you like that? Typical of a kid!

LOUISE: I've been wanting to say this—

ROSE: Always impatient!

LOUISE: Momma—

ROSE: A few break-in dates don't go too hot so she—

LOUISE *(Grabs the wig out of Rose's hand and throws it away)*: Momma, I am not June! I am not a blonde! I can't do what she did!

HERBIE: She's not asking you to.

LOUISE: Maybe you want to stay in show business—

ROSE: Maybe??

LOUISE: Well, I thought—

ROSE: That's our whole life! What've we been working for ever since you were a baby? . . . Maybe I've been on the wrong track with you and the material, but like the good Lord says, you gotta take the rough with the smooth, Baby. And like I always said, you're lucky—because you don't have to take it alone. Right, Herbie?

HERBIE: Right.

ROSE: You got Herbie for brains; we got you for talent; and you both got me—to yell at.

(She sings)
Wherever we go,
Whatever we do,
We're gonna go through it together.
We may not go far.
But sure as a star,
Wherever we are, it's together!

Wherever I go, I know he goes.
Wherever I go, I know she goes.
No fits, no fights, no feuds and no egos—
Amigos, together!

Through thick and through thin,
All out or all in,
And whether it's win, place or show,
With you for me and me for you
We'll muddle through whatever we do
Together, wherever we go!

(Rose holds out her hands to them. They start to sway together)

ALL:
Wherever we go,
Whatever we do,
We're gonna go through it together.

ROSE:

Wherever we sleep—

LOUISE:

If prices are steep—

HERBIE:

We'll always sleep cheaper together.

ROSE:

Whatever the boat I row, you row—

HERBIE:

A duo!

ROSE:

Whatever the row I hoe, you hoe—

LOUISE:

A trio!

ROSE:

And any IOU I owe, you owe—

HERBIE:

Who, me? Oh,
No, you owe!

LOUISE:

No, we owe—

ALL:

Together!
We all take the bow,

ROSE:

Including the cow,

ALL:

Though business is lousy and slow.

ROSE:
> With Herbie's vim, Louise's verve—

HERBIE, LOUISE:
> Now all we need is someone with nerve—

ROSE *(Giving them a look)*:
> Together—

HERBIE, LOUISE:
> Together—

ROSE:
> Wherever—

HERBIE, LOUISE:
> Wherever—

ALL:
> Together wherever we go!

ROSE:
> If I start to dance,

HERBIE, LOUISE:
> We both start to dance,

ALL:
> And sometimes by chance we're together.

ROSE:
> If I sing B flat—ohhhh—

LOUISE:
> We both sing B flat—ohhhh—

HERBIE:
> We all can be flat—ohhhh—

ALL:
> Together!

HERBIE *(Twirling a pie plate)*:
> Whatever the trick, we can do it!

LOUISE *(Twirling a pie plate)*:
> With teamwork we're bound to get through it!

ROSE *(Twirling a third pie plate)*:
> There really isn't anything to it—
> You do it.
>
> *(They toss the plates in the air as if to catch them—the trick is a disaster)*
>
> I knew it—

ALL:
> We blew it—
> Together!
> We go in a group,
> We tour in a troupe,
> We land in the soup
> But we know:
> The things we do, we do by threes,
> A perfect team—
>
> *(Louise heads off in the wrong direction)*

ROSE:
> No, this way, Louise!
> Together—

HERBIE, LOUISE:
> Wherever—

ALL:
> Together wherever we go!
>
> *(Agnes enters with letters)*

AGNES: Here are the letters, Madam Rose.

ROSE: That's a good girl. Now go to bed, Agnes.

AGNES: Now that I'm an actress, it's Amanda.

ROSE: Whatever it is, go to bed.

AGNES: Could I please ask Herbie a question first?

HERBIE: Sure.

AGNES: Herbie . . . do you think we'll ever work again?

ROSE: Of course we will!

HERBIE: I'll get us a booking, Amanda.

AGNES: Thank you, Herbert. *(Turns to go, then sees the wig)* Oh, Louise, your hair!

LOUISE: It's yours if you want it.

AGNES: Gee, I always wanted to be a blonde!

ROSE *(Taking the wig from her)*: Then get some peroxide and a toothbrush. Wigs are expensive.

(Agnes goes off. Rose looks at the wig)

You know, we could get a nice refund on this—if we'd ever paid for it.

HERBIE: How about getting a gallon of peroxide and a carton of toothbrushes?

ROSE: What for?

HERBIE: Make 'em all blondes!

ROSE: I was only joking, Herbie.

HERBIE: So was I, honey.

LOUISE: But why not do it?

ROSE: They're children, Louise!

LOUISE: They're young girls, Momma. With blond hair, they could be pretty young girls.

HERBIE: With a stretch of imagination, they might be. It'd sure jazz up the act and make it easier to sell. We could call it, Madam Rose's Blonde Babies.

ROSE: Baby Blondes!

LOUISE: Nothing with babies.

HERBIE: Hollywood Blondes.

LOUISE: Yes!

ROSE: All blondes except you—because you're the star!

LOUISE: If I'm the star, it should be: *Louise* and Her Hollywood Blondes.

ROSE *(Looks at her—then)*: *Rose* Louise and Her Hollywood Blondes.

LOUISE: O.K.

ALL *(Singing)*:
Through thick and through thin,
All out or all in
And whether it's win, place or show,
With you for me and me for you
We'll muddle through whatever we do
Together, wherever we go!

(The lights dim out)

Scene Two

The placards change to read:

"THE BOTTOM"

WICHITA

Backstage. At one side, there is a theatre dressing room. Upstage is the back of the curtain on the stage of the burlesque theatre.

During the scene, snatches of brassy music come from the "stage." Right now, Agnes and three or four other Girls in the act come in. Each is awed; each carries bags, props, part of the cow; and each has hair of the same, exact hideous shrieking shade of white blond.

AGNES *(In happy awe)*: It's a real live theatre!

MAN'S VOICE *(Off)*: Let in the traveler!

MARJORIE MAY *(Looking off)*: With a real live stage! Don't you love it?

AGNES: Oh, Marjorie May, we've arrived at last!

(They squeal and hug each other as Louise—in slacks—enters from the alley, also carrying bags, props and the cow's head)

DOLORES: Louise, look!

AGNES: A real live theatre!

MAN *(Off)*: Will you kill them floods?

LOUISE *(Happily)*: It's just like opening day rehearsals used to be! Oh, Momma's going to love it!

PASTEY *(Off)*: Will you shut your hole?

AGNES *(Shocked)*: She isn't going to love that!

MARJORIE MAY *(Pointing to the silhouette of a stripper behind the upstage curtain)*: Or *that!*

AGNES: What kind of a act is that?

PASTEY *(Off)*: O.K., jailbait! *(He enters: a young snot, with clipboard and pencil)* You the Hollywood Blondes?

LOUISE: Yes. I'm—

PASTEY: You're late.

LOUISE: Well, our car broke down and—

PASTEY: Skip it. Some of you dogs can use this dressing room, and the rest of you the one past it. The first one you share with Tessie Tura, the Texas Twirler—

LOUISE: My mother doesn't—

PASTEY: The second with Mazeppa, Revolution in Dance. Shake it up. *(Starts to go, then turns back)* So you're the act that's supposed to keep the cops out. Boy, you must be lousy!

(He exits. A moment of deflation. Then—)

LOUISE: It's a real live theatre, all right.

AGNES: He reminds me of my brother.

LOUISE: Don't start sniveling, Amanda. Take the cow and anything else you can carry in there. Marjorie May, you take the other girls into the second room and start unpacking.

(She starts with props and bags for the dressing room. The others pick up their stuff and exit upstage. Thus, all their backs are turned and they do not see two girls who enter to get a gilded spear from a stack leaning against the corridor wall. Each of these bored females wears a gladiator helmet, gladiator boots and carries a large shield in front of her. As they cross up to go to the "stage," we see that the shield is the only thing that covers them.)

They are nude. In the dressing room, Louise and Agnes have started to hang up costumes)

AGNES: Oooh, look at this! *(She is holding up a jeweled G-string, which she proceeds to try on as a necklace)* That Tessie Tura must be a very fancy lady!

LOUISE *(Trying to clean a messy dressing table)*: She must also be a pig!

(Rose enters through the alley door, carrying more bags and props)

ROSE: Louise?

LOUISE: In here, Momma. *(Goes to the door)* Let me help you.

ROSE *(Looking around)*: Baby, we're back in a theatre! We're back in a real theatre!

LOUISE: Momma, where's Herbie?

ROSE: He went around front to check our billing. Louise, I need you here to help me with the rest of the things. *(To the Stagehand, who crosses)* Good morning!

STAGEHAND: Jesus. *(Exits)*

(Rose turns back, stops dead and her mouth drops open. Louise turns and she gapes too. One hand on the edge of the dressing room, throwing wild bumps savagely, is Tessie Tura, a blowsy stripper wearing almost nothing besides a G-string, which does not bump with her. She looks up, during her exercises)

TESSIE: It ain't weighted right, goddamit.

(Mazeppa—a pseudo-exotic grand stripper dressed as Queen of the Gladiators—writhes past Tessie to get her spear from the wall)

It scratches hell outa me and it just don't bump when I do.

MAZEPPA: Maybe there's something wrong with your bumper. *(She exits)*

TESSIE: Big joke. *(To Rose)* I'm out there bumpin' my brains off with no action and she's bein' witty! *(To Agnes, who is gaping*

74

at her from the dressing room doorway) Hey you with the neck! I paid six bucks for that G-string. Back where you found it!

AGNES: Yes, ma'am.

(She curtsies and scurries back in as Tessie goes off. Rose looks at Louise)

ROSE *(Low)*: Get the bags. Get the cow. Get the props.

LOUISE: Now, Momma—

ROSE: You don't know what kind of people are out there on that stage. You don't know what kind of a theatre this is.

LOUISE: Yes I do. It's a house of burlesque.

ROSE: A house of burlesque. Do you know what that is? Filth, that's what! I tell you, when your friend Herbie shows his face—

LOUISE: Momma, I'm sure Herbie didn't know—

ROSE *(Picking up the props, etc., which keep dropping)*: Not much, he didn't know! Agnes!

LOUISE: He got the booking over the telephone—

ROSE: Agnes!

LOUISE: We were all so happy—

ROSE *(Storming to the dressing-room door)*: AGNES, DAM-MIT!

AGNES: Madam Rose, you know my name is—

ROSE: Your name is Agnes and I want you and the other girls out of this hell hole in two seconds flat.

AGNES: But, Madam—

ROSE: March!

AGNES: Yes, ma'am.

(She comes out. Rose goes inside and starts to pack up what has been unpacked)

LOUISE *(To Agnes)*: Wait in the other room.

(Agnes disappears behind the dressing room as Louise goes in)

75

ROSE: You take the rear end of the cow, I'll take the front and what bags we can't carry, your friend Herbie can damn well pick up and carry himself.

(Louise shuts the door. Rose turns and looks at Louise leaning against it. Her voice is low and cold)

Now you listen to me, Louise. Just because you think your friend Herbie can do no wrong—

LOUISE: This has nothing to do with Herbie.

ROSE: You don't know what burlesque is.

LOUISE: Yes I—

ROSE: NO YOU DON'T. No daughter of mine is going to work in burlesque. And no daughter of any woman I know—

LOUISE: Then where *are* we going to work?

ROSE: I'd rather starve!

LOUISE: Momma, how much money do we have? Including what's left of their allowances, how much money do we have?

ROSE: Something'll turn up.

LOUISE: It *has* turned up and *this is it!* We're flat broke, Momma. We've *got* to take this job . . . Even if you wanted to quit and go home, we'd have to take it.

(Rose stops in the act of taking a costume off a hook. A pause. Then abruptly, heavily, she sits)

ROSE: I had a dream . . .

LOUISE: Momma . . .

ROSE: You'll like this one. I had it over a week ago, only I didn't want to tell. I was home in Seattle, and the cow came into my room. But she wasn't dancing and smiling this time. She was wheezing and sad-like. She came over to the bed and looked at me and she said: "Rose, move over."

LOUISE: I'm sorry, Momma.

ROSE *(Smiles)*: Why? She didn't ask you to move over.

LOUISE: I mean I'm sorry I'm not good enough. In the act.

ROSE: Oh, it's the act that ain't good enough, Baby. Or something.

(Herbie hurries in through the alley door)

HERBIE: Rose?

LOUISE *(Opens the dressing-room door)*: In here, Herbie.

HERBIE *(Runs in)*: Rose, I didn't know, believe me.

ROSE: I do, honey. What the hell! The money's good, it's only two weeks, and maybe by that time, something'll turn up. Right?

LOUISE: Right.

HERBIE: You're a nice girl, Rose. Thank you.

ROSE: Well—that's show business. *(She starts to unpack again)*

LOUISE: One good thing: I'll bet we got top billing.

HERBIE: Well—actually they kind of had us lost in the middle. I thought last was better, so it says: "*And* Rose Louise and Her Hollywood Blondes." And I'm making them put a box around it.

ROSE: Forget the box, Herbie.

LOUISE: But, Momma, if—

ROSE: You don't know what they say in the business. But Herbie does. They say when a vaudeville act plays in burlesque, that means it's all washed up. *(Pause)* Herbie . . . nothin's gonna turn up for us, is it?

HERBIE: No.

ROSE: I guess it is a pretty rotten act.

HERBIE: It ain't the act, honey. I been telling you, vaudeville's dead . . . stone cold dead.

ROSE: Well—we sure as hell tried!

HERBIE: You sure as hell did. Right?

LOUISE: Right.

HERBIE: Well, I better get the cues ready. *(He goes to the door)*

ROSE: Herbie—how about marrying me?

HERBIE *(Turns around. A moment. Then, casually)*: Sure!

ROSE: I love you, you know.

HERBIE: I know.

LOUISE: Do it today!

ROSE: Not while we're in burlesque!

HERBIE: The day we close.

ROSE: It's a deal. *(They shake hands and suddenly kiss)* I do, Herbie, I do.

HERBIE: So do I, Rose.

(Pastey barges in. During the following, Tessie appears in the corridor)

PASTEY: Hey, Rose Louise, where the hell's your music and light cues?

HERBIE: I'll be right with you.

PASTEY *(Snotty)*: You Rose Louise?

HERBIE: Yeah, I'm Rose Louise.

PASTEY: Things're looking up. Well, I got a show to open, Rose Louise, so move your ass.

(Before Pastey can get out, Herbie has grabbed him, whirled him around and cracked him in the face. Then, holding him by the scruff of his neck—)

HERBIE: Listen, you little punk. For the next two weeks, you're gonna speak like a Sunday School teacher. You have something in this theatre you probably never saw before. A lady. *(Points him toward Rose)* Look at her. That is a lady. *(Points him toward Louise)* That is also a lady. Every girl in this damn act is a lady, you understand?

PASTEY: Yes, sir.

HERBIE: Now get on stage and I'll give you those cues when I'm ready.

PASTEY: Yes, sir. Excuse me, ma'am.

(He goes out and off. Rose kisses Herbie. He goes out but is stopped in the corridor by Tessie)

TESSIE: Oh, sir? Won't you give *me* your protection? I'm a lady, too! *(On the last, a vivacious grind and bump. The bumper flips)* Hey! The goddam thing worked! *(She goes into the dressing room as Herbie goes off)* If you ladies will excuse me—

ROSE: We're very busy.

TESSIE: In *my* dressing room.

ROSE: In *your* dress—

LOUISE *(Overlapping)*: Momma—

TESSIE: You're damn right. And I don't like sharing it any more than you do. Particularly with a troupe of professional virgins.

ROSE: We are not—

TESSIE: All right, so you're acrobats.

ROSE: We happen to be headliners from the Orpheum Circuit. We were booked into this theatre by mistake.

TESSIE: Weren't we all! *(Reaching for a costume Rose has unpacked)* Say! Who made that?

LOUISE: I did. I make all our costumes.

TESSIE: My! Look at them ladylike little stitches! That miserable broad who makes my gowns must be usin' a fish hook!

LOUISE: What do you pay her?

TESSIE: Twenty-five bucks a gown and I provide the material.

ROSE: Thirty.

TESSIE: She's new in the business!

ROSE: Thirty.

TESSIE: Who're you? Her mother?

ROSE: Yes.

TESSIE: Thirty. I'll get the material after the matinée.

ROSE: It's a deal. *(To Louise)* Where's your toreador costume?

LOUISE: The girls must have it in the dressing room with them.

ROSE: God knows what else they've got in there with them! *(She exits)*

TESSIE: You know, from the way that dame walks, she would have made a damn good stripper in her day.

79

(A burly man, Cigar, the manager, enters)

CIGAR: Hey, Tessie, I'm short a talking woman.

TESSIE: Tough titty.

CIGAR: The new comic won't use a chorus girl.

TESSIE: Then let him use Mazeppa. *(To Louise)* Everyone else has. *(She laughs at her joke)*

CIGAR: Now you know Mazeppa's got her Gladiator Ballet just before his spot.

TESSIE: Cut the ballet. It stinks anyway.

CIGAR: Be a sport. I'm in a bind.

TESSIE: You're always in a bind in this flea-bitten trap. I'm a strip woman, slob. I don't do no scenes. Now screw! *(To Louise)* You ever hear of a strip woman playing scenes? Well, you play stock in a dump like this, you gotta expect to be insulted.

CIGAR: The work is steady, ain't it?

TESSIE: But you bring in a new star for each show, don't you?

CIGAR: Tessie, it's just a few lines—

TESSIE: Fat boy, save your bad breath.

CIGAR: I'll give you ten bucks extra.

TESSIE: Nah.

LOUISE *(As Rose returns)*: I can read lines.

CIGAR: Who're you?

LOUISE: Rose Louise. Of Rose Louise and Her Hollywood Blondes.

ROSE: Wait a minute. What kind of lines?

CIGAR: You in her act?

ROSE: Well, not exactly.

CIGAR: Shut up. *(To Louise)* How are your legs?

TESSIE: Great! And I'll learn her the scenes.

CIGAR: O.K. Ten bucks. *(He goes)*

LOUISE: It's money, Momma.

ROSE *(Going to Tessie)*: What is she going to be saying out there on that stage?

TESSIE: The same burlesque crap that's been said since the Year One. Say, where you been all your life?

ROSE *(Proudly)*: Playing vaudeville.

TESSIE: Where? In the Vatican?

ROSE: You name a big city and we've played it!

LOUISE: My grandpa says we've covered the country like Gypsies!

TESSIE: Yeah? Well, you may be a Gypsy, Rose Louise—say, that ain't a bad name if you ever take up stripping—

ROSE: She won't!

TESSIE: No! But you'll let her feed lines to a bum comic for a lousy ten bucks a week!

ROSE: That's training: she's going to be an actress! This is only temporary! After we finish here, she goes right back to vaudeville! *(She turns away—and sees Louise's look. Embarrassed, she exits)*

TESSIE *(Quietly)*: Back to vaudeville, my eye. There ain't any vaudeville left except burlesque.

LOUISE: We know.

TESSIE: *You* know. You better wise *her* up.

LOUISE *(Sudden burst)*: She's wise! She's a damn sight wiser than any of you!

TESSIE *(Shrugs)*: Like mother, like daughter. O. K. Say, whose feelings did I hurt? Yours or hers?

LOUISE *(Smiles)*: Neither. We'll both be fine.

TESSIE: I hope so, because sharing a dressing room is like sleeping together. And if you don't get along with—

(Mazeppa comes storming on with Electra, another stripper)

MAZEPPA: Miss Tura, I'll thank you not to give the boss any notion that I would ever play scenes. And one more disparaging remark about my ballet will find this bugle right up your—

TESSIE: Please: there's a lady present!

MAZEPPA: Where?

TESSIE: Open your eyes instead of your mouth. Gypsy, meet Miss Mazeppa—and Miss Electra.

ELECTRA: Say, you're even younger than I was when I began stripping.

LOUISE: I'm not going to strip.

MAZEPPA *(Belligerent)*: Something wrong with stripping?

LOUISE: No. I just meant I don't have any talent.

TESSIE: You think they have? I myself of course was a ballerina. But take it from me, to be a stripper all you need to have is no talent.

MAZEPPA: You'll pardon me, but to have no talent is not enough. What you need is an idea that makes your strip special.

(During the following number, each of the three strippers demonstrates the gimmick that has made her a "star." Mazeppa sings)

You can pull all the stops out
Till they call the cops out,
Grind your behind till you're banned,
But you gotta get a gimmick
If you wanna get a hand.

You can sacrifice your sacro
Workin' in the back row,
Bump in a dump till you're dead.
Kid, you gotta get a gimmick
If you wanna get ahead.

You can—!, you can—!, you can—!!!
That's how burlesque was born.
So I—! and I—! and I—!!!
But I do it with a horn!

(She demonstrates: bumping and grinding like mad while she blows army calls on her bugle)

Once I was a schlepper,
Now I'm Miss Mazeppa
With my Revolution in Dance.
You gotta have a gimmick
If you wanna have a chance!!!

ELECTRA *(Singing)*:

She can—!, she can—!, she can—!!!
They'll never make her rich.
Me, I—! and I—! and I—!!!
But I do it with a switch!

(She demonstrates: punctuating her bumps and grinds with electric lights which illuminate her strategic points)

I'm electrifying,
And I'm not even trying.
I never have to sweat to get paid.
'Cause if you got a gimmick,
Gypsy girl, you've got it made.

TESSIE *(Singing)*:

All them—!s and them—!s and them—!!!s
Ain't gonna spell success.
Me, I—! and! I—! and I—!!!
But I do it with finesse!

(And she demonstrates: a broken-down version of ballet climaxed with the same eternal bumps and grinds)

Dressy Tessie Tura
Is so much demurer
Than all them other ladies because
You gotta get a gimmick
If you wanna get applause!

ALL:

Do somethin' special;
Anything that's fresh'll

Earn you a big fat cigar.
You're more than just a mimic
When you got a gimmick—
Take a look how different we are!

(They bump and grind: what else?)

ELECTRA:

If you wanna make it,
Shake it till you break it.

TESSIE:

If you wanna grind it,
Wait till you've refined it.

MAZEPPA:

If you wanna bump it,
Bump it with a trumpet!

ALL:

Get yourself a gimmick
And you too
Can be a star!

(The lights black out)

Scene Three

The scene is backstage.

STAGEHAND *(To Pastey, who is crossing)*: Kill the floods and bring in number four!

PASTEY: I tole ya we ain't usin' number four this show, ya pinhead!

HERBIE *(Runs on with a little bouquet)*: Hey, you seen Amanda?

PASTEY: She must be packin'. Ain't your act through today?

HERBIE *(Joyously)*: You bet it is! Through—finished—over!

(Agnes comes on with a suitcase. Herbie crosses to her)

PASTEY *(To the Stagehand)*: Will you kill number four? *(He exits)*

HERBIE *(To Agnes)*: I've been hunting for you. Here. *(He gives her the bouquet)*

AGNES: Oh, Herbie, it's like for a funeral!

HERBIE: It's for the wedding! Madam Rose and I want you to be bridesmaid, Amanda.

AGNES: It's Agnes again.

HERBIE *(Hugs her)*: You'll be happier as Agnes, Amanda. *(Dashing off)* See you out front.

TESSIE *(Runs on)*: Oh, you're leaving!

AGNES: I have to go home and let my hair grow out.

TESSIE: Ya poor kid.

PASTEY *(Off)*: Tessie!

TESSIE: Well—for the last time: *(Doing a grind)* Meet ya round the corner *(Agnes joins in)* in a half-hour.

(Agnes breaks down on Tessie's bosom)

PASTEY: TESSIE!

TESSIE: TESSIE! I'm coming, ya creep!

(She hurries to the wings leading to the "stage." A farewell wave to Agnes, a lift to her sagging bosoms—and she floats off like a ballerina)

(The lights black out)

Scene Four

The dressing room looks emptier. Most of Rose's belongings have been packed.

The lights are different. The corridor is darker but streaked with colored light coming from the "stage," where the show is on. Herbie—in a different suit—Rose and Louise—in coats—are finishing packing. Rose is very subdued; Herbie is very up; Louise keeps watching Rose.

HERBIE *(To Rose)*: Why aren't you nervous? I've never been so nervous in my whole life!

LOUISE *(Hands Rose a baton)*: You've never been married before.

HERBIE: Well, your mother's never been married like she's going to be this time. For keeps and forever—to me! Ain't you a *little* nervous, honey!

ROSE: Sure.

HERBIE *(Admiring the marriage license)*: Say, the minister doesn't keep this, does he? I want to have it framed. Framed and hanging in our living room.

LOUISE *(Holding the cow head)*: What about this Momma?

ROSE: Take it.

HERBIE: Rose—

LOUISE *(Putting the cow head on the suitcase)*: We can hang her up in the living room, too, Herbie. Over the mantelpiece.

HERBIE: Rose honey, it ain't that I don't know what you're feeling. Or that I don't know I oughta shut up. But I'm so goddam happy, I can't!

(Cigar and Pastey enter the corridor. Their dialogue and Herbie's are simultaneous. Rose listens to Herbie)

I'm finally getting everything I wanted! Even a fancy ceremony with bridesmaids. Of course, what the minister's going to say when he gets a load of all that hair, I don't know. But the hell with him!

(Rose's attention shifts to the hall)

All he's gotta say is, Do you, Rose, take him, Herbie?

CIGAR: I don't know why the hell I stay in this business. If it ain't one damn headache, it's another!

PASTEY: Ssh! They'll hear you out front.

CIGAR: It's my theatre, ain't it? Let 'em! Last show, no talking woman. Show before that, no second banana. If that crazy broad wasn't here, why did you start the performance?

PASTEY: She don't go on till next to closing, and she said she was only goin' next door to the drugstore.

(Herbie and then Louise become aware that Rose is standing dead still, listening. They stand, watching her, tense, afraid)

CIGAR: What'd they arrest her for? Shoplifting?

PASTEY: No, soliciting.

CIGAR: She always was greedy. Well, cut the spot.

HERBIE: Honey, do you think we can invite the minister for a drink after?

PASTEY: It's the star strip!

CIGAR: Cut it.

PASTEY: They'll yell murder if it's only the same bags they've been seeing the last eight weeks. The star's the novelty!

CIGAR: Whaddya want me to do? Let you strip?

(Rose throws down whatever she is holding and runs out of the dressing room into the corridor)

ROSE: My daughter can do it. *(They look at her. She steps back, as though afraid of herself)* Rose Louise.

PASTEY: Since when?

ROSE: Since she's been here to see how little there is to it.

CIGAR: She didn't look bad in them scenes.

ROSE: She'll look great in her own gowns.

PASTEY: What's the gimmick?

CIGAR: She's young. And you got any better ideas?

PASTEY *(As he exits)*: Well, she better get ready right damn now.

ROSE: It's the star spot.

CIGAR: You telling me?

ROSE: That means the star salary.

CIGAR: If we keep her.

ROSE: You will. She's going to be wonderful

(Cigar goes off as Rose runs excitedly into the dressing room and begins opening a suitcase. Herbie and Louise stand dead still, watching)

I knew something would turn up! Where's that dress you were gonna make for Tessie? It'll work perfect for you! . . . *(Gets the dress out)* Well, get your makeup on, there ain't much time! . . . Oh, silly, you're not really gonna strip! All you'll do is walk around the stage in time to the music and drop a shoulder strap at the end. *(Takes out the makeup)* You're a lady—like Herbie says you are! You just parade so grand they'll think it's a favor if you even show them your knee—Louise, it's the star spot! I promised my daughter we'd be a star! *(Still, Louise just stands)* Baby, it's all right to walk out when they *want* you. But you can't walk out when after all these rotten years, we're still a flop. That's quitting. We can't quit because we're a flop! Louise *(A burst)* don't be like June. Just do this, and then we can walk away proud because we made it! Maybe only in burlesque, maybe only in second-rate burlesque at that—but let's walk away a star!

(Louise unbuttons her coat. Rose hugs her, then rummages for the dress as Louise begins quickly to get ready)

I guess there ain't time to finish the dress, but we can pin it easy. Hey, here's some material for extra panels! Didn't I always say you were born lucky? You can unpin the panels and drop 'em every once in a while so they'll think you're taking something off.

(Slowly, Herbie folds up the license and walks out of the room, and disappears in the corridor. Louise is making up feverishly)

Not too much makeup, Baby. Young and girlish. Pure. Don't smear that junk all over your face like they do. You just keep your mouth the way the Lord made it . . . No rouge. No beauty marks. You be a lady: grand, elegant . . . with a classy, ladylike walk. My God! Shoes! . . . Well, we can use the old silver ones we borrowed from Tessie. *(She takes them from her own suitcase)* They'll do for this performance . . . Come on. Get into 'em. *(As Louise does)* Oh, no—your hair's wrong. You can't let it just hang like spaghetti. Put it up! Like Momma's! It's got to have class! Puff it out in front. Thank God, the Lord gave us good color— and that you washed it this morning . . . Say, do you think we should put a couple of feathers in? *(Tries some)* No, that's what they all do. *(Tosses them aside)* Jewelry? No. Let Tessie and the others wear all the vulgar junk they want.

PASTEY *(Rushes in)*: She almost ready? She goes on in five minutes.

ROSE *(Pushing him out)*: She'll be there—she'll be there! Come on, get into the dress.

(Louise exits through another door, presumably leading into a bathroom, to change into the strip dress. Rose picks up a pair of long white gloves)

Whose are these? Oh—my wedding present from Tessie. Good for a lady. Wear 'em . . . Now, what else? . . . Music! *(Flips through sheet music in the suitcase)* "Spanish"— "Cow"? *(Shakes her head)* No. Say, you can do June's "Let Me Entertain You" number! I'll mark it for the conductor to repeat two choruses slow—no, two and a half choruses, and sing out, Louise! You just walk and dip . . . you're a lady; you make 'em beg for more—and then *don't* give it to them! . . . Now—have I forgotten anything? Anything else?

(On the last, Herbie enters the dressing room. He is almost shaking with anger and his effort to control it)

Where you been? Out front?

HERBIE: No, I got sick to my stomach, and threw up.

ROSE: But you feel better now.

HERBIE: No.

ROSE: Herbie—I just had to.

HERBIE: That's why I'm leaving.

ROSE: I apologize.

HERBIE: No, let me. For my resemblance to a mouse. No: to a worm—the way I've crawled after you. No more, Rose. I won't. I was even going to crawl away from you—because my stomach started to turn over at the idea of coming back and telling you we're finished.

ROSE: Tell me tomorrow—after we're married.

HERBIE: We're never getting married, Rose.

ROSE: We certainly are! First thing in the morning, we'll—

HERBIE: *Never!* Not if you went down on your knees and begged. I still love you—but all the vows from here to doomsday . . . they couldn't make you a wife. I want a wife, Rose. I'm going to be a man if it kills me.

ROSE *(Angrily)*: So you're killing *me!*

HERBIE: Nobody can kill you.

ROSE: You're jealous, that's what you are! Like every man I've ever known! Jealous—because my girls come first. Well, they always did and they always will!

HERBIE: Then why did June leave?

ROSE: I don't wanna hear her name!

HERBIE: She didn't want the act any more than Louise wants this!

ROSE: Louise does!

HERBIE: She'll leave like June did!

ROSE: Never! She's gonna be a star.

HERBIE: She's gonna be a star! If it kills *you and her,* she's gonna be a star *someplace! She's* gonna be a star. Where are *you* gonna be, Rose? Where are you gonna be when *she* gets married?

ROSE: She won't be getting married for years—she's a baby!

HERBIE: Sure!

ROSE: Anyway, her career will always come first. *(She sits, looks over the music defiantly)*

HERBIE: That's right. That-is-right. *(He picks up his suitcase, and starts out)*

ROSE: Herbie . . . why does everybody walk out?

HERBIE: Maybe Louise won't.

ROSE: Don't leave, Herbie . . . I need you.

HERBIE: . . . What for?

ROSE: A million things.

HERBIE: Just one would be better. Goodbye, honey. Be a good girl.

(He goes out the door. Music starts)

ROSE: You go to hell!

(Rose sits staring and Pastey runs in)

PASTEY: Get her music to the conductor and you better stand
by me for the light cues. I just hope you know what you're
doing.

(Pastey races out)

ROSE *(Singing)*:
Lucky, you're a man who likes children—
  That's an important sign.
Lucky, I'm a woman with children—
Funny,
  Small and funny—

*(Rose get up and slowly walks to the white gloves. She has them
in her hand, and is staring at them as Louise comes out and
takes the gloves from her. Rose watches her start to put them on,
then speaks quietly, as though dazed)*

ROSE: I'll get the music to the conductor. Just remember—
you're a lady *(With anguished determination)* And you-are-
going-to-be-a-star!

*(Music in hand, she walks out, leaving Louise alone before a
long mirror in the dressing room. As she draws on the white
gloves, the music ends and the light in the corridor goes very
dark. There is a soft glow on the mirror as dark figures scurry
through the corridor outside saying: "Let's watch from the
wings." "No, I'm going out front." "What's she gonna do?"
"She isn't the type." "She'll quit halfway through." "How do
you know?" "She'll never make it." "Come on, let's get a good
place." "I'm scared for her." During this, the dressing room has
been rolling off, leaving only the mirror. The only light on the
stage is the glow of the mirror bulbs; the only figure is Louise.
She looks at herself, goes close to the mirror to check her makeup,
then suddenly stops. She touches her body lightly, moves back,
straightens up and stares at her reflection. Very softly—)*

LOUISE: Momma...I'm pretty...I'm a pretty girl, Momma!

(Very grand, very proud, very beautiful, she turns from the mirror and begins to walk away from it, as though she were going in the direction of the "stage." The mirror moves off, the lights come up and we are "on the stage." The curtain is upstage; strip music can be heard, a dim stripper can be seen through the curtain. Rose, who is peering through, turns around and sees Louise)

ROSE *(Softly)*: You look beautiful!

TESSIE *(Runs on with an old fur stole which she wraps around Louise)*: For luck, honey!

ROSE: Are you nervous, Baby?

LOUISE: ...What?

ROSE: I said, Are you nervous?

LOUISE: No, Mother.

(The offstage music ends; there is applause as the weary stripper comes on from behind the curtain, looks at Louise and goes off. Pastey grabs a microphone)

PASTEY: Wichita's one and only Burlesque Theatre presents—

LOUISE *(Nervous after all)*: Momma—

PASTEY: Miss—Gypsy—Rose—Lee!

TESSIE *(Correcting him angrily)*: Louise!

(But he shrugs. Everyone exits but Louise, who stands alone before the curtain. A roll of the drum and lights reveal the curtain as a scrim. Through it, we can see the glow of the strippers' runway. Another drum roll: the curtains part and Louise steps forward. Another drum roll: a spotlight hits her and her head goes back as though she has been blinded. Blinding floodlights then shine directly into the eyes of the audience; then a total blackout. When the lights go on again, Louise is downstage, facing the audience before a curtain the exact replica of the one upstage. Her head is back a bit, her eyes closed, the spotlight bright on her. The

small burlesque band in the pit begins "Let Me Entertain You."
Louise can barely start singing. Rose, from the wings, calls out)

ROSE: Sing out, Louise!

(Louise sings a little louder, a little truer. She looks around at
the men out front: They like her. Her voice is stronger as she
finishes. What now? She begins to walk around a little
awkwardly)

CIGAR *(From the wings)*: Do something!

(Louise shoots a panicky look to Rose in the wings)

ROSE: Dip! Dip!

(Louise does. But that's not enough)

CIGAR: Take something off!

ROSE: A glove! Give 'em a glove!

(Louise does. But now what?)

Say something!
LOUISE: Hello—

(A nice laugh from out front. She smiles)

—everybody. My name is—Gypsy—Rose—Lee! *(She's en-*
joying this now. A sexy look to a man out front) What's yours—
sir? *(Now she has it)* Mr. Conductor—if you please! *(And*
from the way she walks, it is clear she is on her way. A dropped
shoulder strap just before she exits is her confirming punctuation)

(The lights on the curtain change. The placards scroll to read

DETROIT

and an announcer's voice comes over)

ANNOUNCER: Detroit's Diamond Burlesque is happy to pres-

ent a new jewel in its glittering crown—Miss Gypsy—
Rose—Lee!

*(And out she comes in a glittering, revealing dress and a rose in
her hair. She is poised now and her humor is beginning to shine
through. As she walks downstage:)*

LOUISE: I'm beginning to like this! *(She stops and begins to toy
with her dress and her body. She speaks in a syncopated rhythm)*
My mother—who got me into this business—
(She is pulling up her dress)
Always told me
Make them beg for more—
(Drops the dress)
And then, don't give it to them!
But I'm not my mothah!
Beg!

*(Change of lights and music for a montage of changing placards
and overlapping voices:*

PHILADELPHIA

BOSTON

and last:

MINSKY'S
NEW YORK

ANNOUNCER: Philadelphia, the city of Brotherly Love, brings
all you brothers a sister to make you leave home!
SECOND ANNOUNCER: Boston's World Famous Howard Burlesque has no need of Paul Revere to announce the arrival at
the home of Liberty of the Belle that rings out for one and
all—
THIRD ANNOUNCER: Minsky's World Famous Burlesque takes
great pride and pleasure in presenting the Queen of the

Strip Tease, the incomparable Miss Gypsy Rose Lee in our Salute to the Garden of Eden!

(The curtain opens on a garish version of the garden with semi-nudes who come down from sequined trees, grinding away like mad and singing—along with multi-dubbed additional angel voices—as they throw apples to the audience. At the peak, two almost nude satyrs bring on a big, jeweled apple out of which steps Gypsy: elegant, mischievous, glittering like a real diamond in the Five and Dime. Crescendo, then:)

LOUISE: Pack up your apples, girls, and back to the trees.

(As the girls depart, the curtain closes in front of them and Louise chatters to the audience as, accompanied by percussion only, she walks around the stage, stripping off gloves, etc.)

Bonsoir, messieurs—et messieurs. Je m'appelle Gypsy Rose Lee *et je suis dans le jardin de ma mère,* Eve. And that concludes my entire performance—in French. I've been too busy learning Greek. Some man called me an ecdysiast. Do you know what means? Do you? Do you?

(Spot hits man in audience)

Oh, he does. Where were you last night? He's embarrassed. Don't be embarrassed. I like men without hair. An ecdysiast is one who—or that which—sheds its skin. In vulgar parlance, a stripper. But I'm not a stripper. At these prices, I'm an ecdysiast!

(She has seemingly taken everything off and now grabs the curtain to cover herself as she drags it across the stage, singing the last eight bars of "Let Me Entertain You". On the last note, the light go out except for a blue spot on Louise. She drops the curtain and throws a bump and a kiss. Blackout)

97

Scene Five

The placards change to read:

"MOTHER'S DAY"
MINSKY'S

A dressing room.

The basic crumminess of the room is all but hidden by the trappings its occupant has installed: gleaming bottles; a nude statue festooned with feathers and a rhinestone G-string; souvenirs; costumes, etc.

Rose is hammering a spike into the wall, as she talks to Renée, the maid, who barely listens. During the following, Rose hangs the cow's head up on the spike.

ROSE: Sure I saw that sign! If I can read the fine print in our contracts, I can certainly read letters two feet high: "THE MOTHER OF MISS GYPSY ROSE LEE IS NOT ALLOWED BACKSTAGE AT THIS THEATRE." You know what I did with that sign? *(Puts a string of beads on the cow's horn)* I tore it off the wall, spread it on the floor, and set Chowsie III down on it. That dog's a trouper: *she* knew what to do! . . . It'll take more than signs to keep me out of a theatre!

(The door opens and Louise enters in a negligée. She is singing until she sees Rose. And the cow head)

LOUISE That comes down. *(She sits at the dressing table and swiftly sets about repairing her makeup)*

ROSE: You need *something* to remind you your goal was to be a great actress, not a cheap stripper.

LOUISE: June's the actress, Mother. And I'm not a cheap stripper. I'm the highest paid in the business.

ROSE: You won't be ready when vaudeville comes back.

LOUISE: No, I'll be dead. *(Then, indicating the furs she has thrown on a chair)* Renée, tell Sam he can lock up the animals for the night.

ROSE: I'll do it.

LOUISE: Mother, please. *(To Renée)* And bring my press agent in as soon as he gets here.

RENÉE: *Oui, madame. (She goes out with the furs and the cow head)*

ROSE: Since when do you fix your face before you take your bath?

LOUISE: A photographer's coming.

ROSE: Where's he going to photograph you? In the tub?

LOUISE: Eventually.

ROSE *(Shocked)*: Louise!

LOUISE: It's for *Vogue.*

ROSE *(Elated)*: Louise!! Think I ought to freshen up?

LOUISE: They only want me in the tub, Mother.

(The telephone rings)

ROSE: I've got it.

LOUISE *(Beating Rose to it)*: Hello?...*(Intimately)* Hello. No, it's difficult right now.

ROSE: I'm not leaving.

LOUISE: Let's meet at the party...Yes, I promise. *À bientôt.* *(She hangs ups)*

ROSE: *À bien* what?

LOUISE: I guess I am being a little much—but, Momma, I love it.

ROSE: Who's giving the party?

LOUISE: Some friends.

ROSE: In the old days, I was always invited first.

LOUISE: Mother—

ROSE *(Very grandly)*: I wouldn't go even if I *did* have something to wear. I got more important things to do—like thinking up an idea for a new strip for us.

LOUISE: Mother, we're still stuck with that wind machine you bought to *blow* my clothes off. Actually—I'm putting in a new number on Saturday.

ROSE: What is it?

LOUISE: You'll see.

ROSE: I'll see.

LOUISE: Let me surprise you.

ROSE: These days, you're just one big surprise after another. Well, we better go shopping tomorrow for the material for the gown.

LOUISE: I've got a French lesson tomorrow.

ROSE: Oh. Well, I'll go alone. Got any particular color in mind?

LOUISE: Mother—I've already started to make the gown.

ROSE: Oh. Well, I better run your bath for you.

LOUISE: You don't have to. That's what I've got a maid for.

ROSE: LET ME DO SOMETHING, DAMMIT!

LOUISE *(Very quietly)*: What, Mother?

ROSE: A million things. I'm not a baby.

LOUISE: Neither am I.

ROSE: Don't you take that tone to me. Your sister used to get that edge to her voice—

LOUISE: I am not June!

ROSE: You're not Louise, either!

LOUISE: And neither are you!

ROSE: Oh, yes I am! More than you, Miss Gypsy Rose Lee— with your dirty pictures for *Vogue!*

LOUISE: Mother—

ROSE: And your maids and your press agents and your fancy friends with their fancy parties!

LOUISE: They happen—

ROSE: Your loud-mouth mother ain't invited to those goddam parties. They laugh at her!

LOUISE: They don't—

ROSE: THEY DO! And don't think I don't know that's one reason why you don't want me backstage: so I won't hear 'em laugh. Well, it's *them* you oughta keep out, not me! Because they're laughing at you, too! The burlesque queen who speaks lousy French and reads book reviews like they was books!

LOUISE: Turn it off, Mother.

ROSE: You know what you are to them? A circus freak! This year's novelty act! And when the bill is changed—

LOUISE: I SAID TURN IT OFF! *Nobody laughs at me*— because I laugh first! *At* me! ME—from Seattle; me—with no education; me, with no talent—as you've kept reminding me my whole life. Look at me now: a star! Look how I live! Look at my friends! Look where I'm going! I'm not staying in burlesque. I'm moving—maybe up, maybe down—but wherever it is, I'm *enjoying* it! I'm having the time of my life because for the first time, it *is* my life! I love it! I love every second of it and I'll be damned if you're going to take it away from me! I *am* Gypsy Rose Lee! I love her—and if you don't you can clear out *now!*

(A moment: Rose stares at her, stunned. Then a knocking on the door and Renée enters)

RENÉE: Your press agent is here with the photographer.

LOUISE: Tell him I'll be ready in a minute. *(Softly)* Momma, we can't go shouting seven performances of this a week.

ROSE: The whole family shouts: it comes from our living so near the railroad tracks.

LOUISE: I'm getting an ulcer.

ROSE: You think I'm not?

LOUISE: Yes, I think you're not. And if you want an ulcer, Momma, get one of your own. You can't have mine.

ROSE: Everyone has stomach trouble but me!

LOUISE: Mother, you fought your whole life. I wish you could relax now—

ROSE: You need more mascara on your left eye.

LOUISE: *Momma, you have got to let go of me!*

ROSE: Let go?

LOUISE: I'll give you anything you want—

ROSE: You *need* me!

LOUISE: A house, a farm, a school—a dramatic school for kids? You were always great with kids!

ROSE *(Cutting in)*: *I'm a pro!* Not an old work horse you can turn out to pasture just because you think you're riding high on your own!

LOUISE: Momma, no kid does it all on his own but *I am not a kid anymore!* From now on, even if I flop, I flop on my own!

(A knock on the door)

PHIL *(Off)*: Hey, Gyps, what do you say?

ROSE: "So long, Rose," that's what she says. "Don't slam the door as you leave." *(She starts to go, but is pushed aside by the press agent and the photographer who come in. She stands watching)*

PHIL *(As he enters)*: Hi, Rose. Gyps, baby, may I present Monsieur Bougeron-Cochon.

LOUISE: *Enchanté, monsieur.*

BOUGERON-COCHON: *Enchanté.*

PHIL: Let's make with the *oiseau*, kiddies. One before you take the plunge, Gyps. All set . . .

(Louise takes a cheesecake pose)

Fine!

ROSE: All right, miss. But just one thing I want to know. All the working and pushing and fenagling. All the scheming and scrimping and lying awake nights figuring: How do we get from one town to the next? How do we all eat on a buck?

How do I make an act out of nothing? What'd I do it for? You say I fought my whole life. I fought *your* whole life. So now tell me: *What'd I do it for?*

LOUISE *(Quietly, after a long moment)*: I thought you did it for me, Momma.

(Rose stares. Her hands drop to her sides. She turns and quietly goes out)

PHIL: Come on, smile, Gyps. Show us your talent!

(She bares a leg)

That's it!

(The flashbulb explodes)

(The lights black out)

Scene Six

A lone spot picks up Rose as she moves down front.

ROSE: "I thought you did it for me, Momma." "I thought you did it for me, Momma . . . " I thought you made a no-talent ox into a star because you like doing things the hard way, Momma. *(Louder)* And you *haven't* got any talent! Not what *I* call talent, Miss Gypsy Rose Lee!

(The lights now begin to come up)

I made you! And you wanna know why? You wanna know what I did it for?! *(Louder) Because I was born too soon and started too late, that's why!* With what I have in me, I could've been better than ANY OF YOU! What I got in me—what I been holding down inside of me—if I ever let it out, there wouldn't be signs big enough! There wouldn't be lights bright enough! *(Shouting right out to everyone now)* HERE SHE IS, BOYS! HERE SHE IS, WORLD! HERE'S ROSE!!

(She sings)
CURTAIN UP!!!
LIGHT THE LIGHTS!!!

(Speaking as the lights come up on the strippers' runway)
Play it, boys.

(Singing)
You either got it,
or you ain't—
And, boys, I got it!
You like it?

ORCHESTRA: Yeah!

ROSE:
Well, I got it!
Some people got it
   And make it pay,
Some people can't even
   Give it away.
This people's got it
   And this people's spreadin' it around.
You either have it
   Or you've had it.

(Speaking)
Hello, everybody, My name's Rose. What's yours? *(Bumps)*
How d'ya like them egg rolls, Mr. Goldstone?

(Singing)
Hold your hats,
   And hallelujah,
Momma's gonna show it to ya!

(Speaking)
Ready or not, here comes Momma!

(Singing)
Momma's talkin' loud,
Momma's doin' fine,
Momma's gettin' hot,
Momma's goin' strong,
Momma's movin' on,
Momma's all alone,

Momma's doesn't care,
Momma's lettin' loose,
Momma's got the stuff,
Momma's lettin' go—

(Stopping dead as the words hit her)

Momma—
Momma's—

(Shaking off the mood)

Momma's got the stuff,
Momma's got to move,
Momma's got to go—

(Stopping dead again, trying to recover)

Momma—
Momma's—
Momma's gotta let go!

(Stops; after a moment she begins to pace)

Why did I do it?
    What did it get me?
Scrapbooks full of me in the background.
Give 'em love and what does it get you?
What does it get you?
One quick look as each of 'em leaves you.
All your life and what does it get you?
Thanks a lot—and out with the garbage.
They take bows and you're battin' zero.
I had a dream—
I dreamed it for you,
    June,
It wasn't for me, Herbie.
And if it wasn't for me
Then where would you be,

Miss Gypsy Rose Lee!
Well, someone tell me, when is it my turn?
Don't I get a dream for myself?
Startin' now it's gonna be my turn!
Gangway, world,
    Get offa my runway!
Startin' now I bat a thousand.
This time, boys, I'm takin' the bows and
Everything's coming up Rose—
Everything's coming up Roses—
Everything's coming up Roses
This time for me!
For me—
For me—
For me—
For me—
FOR ME!

(She takes her bows. The runway lights go out, the applause dies out, but Rose is still bowing to the triumph in her head. Louise comes on applauding, tall and beautiful in a mink coat over a perfect evening gown. Rose turns, and with an embarrassed smile says—)

Just trying out a few ideas you might want to use . . .

LOUISE *(Quietly)*: You'd really have been something, Mother.

ROSE: Think so?

LOUISE: If you had had someone to push you like I had . . .

ROSE: If I could've been, I would've been. And *that's* show business . . . I guess I did do it for me.

LOUISE: Why, Mother?

ROSE: Just wanted to be noticed.

LOUISE: Like I wanted you to notice me.

(Rose turns and looks at her)

I still do, Momma. *(She holds out her arms to Rose, who hesi-*

tates, then goes into Louise's arms) O.K., Momma . . . O.K., Rose.

(Rose clutches her, then moves away. She forces a smile as she turns back)

ROSE: Say, you look like you should speak French!

LOUISE: You're coming to that party with me.

ROSE: No.

LOUISE: Come on.

ROSE: Like this?

LOUISE: Here. You wear my mink. I've got a stole in the box office.

ROSE: Well—just for an hour or two. Say, this looks better on me than on you! . . . Funny how we can wear the same size.

LOUISE *(A knowing look)*: Especially in mink.

ROSE: You know, I had a dream last night. It was a big poster of a mother and daughter—you know, like the cover of that ladies' magazine.

LOUISE *(Warningly)*: Yes, Mother?

ROSE *(Stops moving)*: Only it was you and me, wearing exactly the same gown. It was an ad for Minsky—and the headline said: *(She traces the name in the air)* MADAM ROSE—

(Louise gives her a look; Rose catches it and, moving her hand up to give Louise top billing, says)

AND HER DAUGHTER, GYPSY!

(Louise laughs and starts off. Rose starts to follow, then turns back: The runway lights come on. She takes an eager step toward them, they go out in her face. A moment, then she turns and goes off)

(The curtain falls)